Barnabas for Children

Barnabas for Children® is a registered word mark
and the logo is a registered device mark of The Bible Reading Fellowship.

Published by
The Bible Reading Fellowship
15 The Chambers, Vineyard
Abingdon OX14 3FE, United Kingdom
Tel: +44 (0)1865 319700
Email: enquiries@brf.org.uk; Website: www.brf.org.uk
BRF is a Registered Charity

ISBN 978 0 85746 353 1
First edition 2015

Copyright © 2015 Anno Domini Publishing
www.ad-publishing.com
Text copyright © 2015 Sally Ann Wright
Illustrations copyright © Honor Ayres, Paola Bertolini Grudina,
Estelle Corke, Frank Endersby, Melanie Florian, Moira Maclean,
Carla Manea, Krisztina Kállai Nagy, Martina Peluso, Heather Stuart

Editorial Director: Annette Reynolds
Art Director: Gerald Rogers
Pre-production Manager: Krystyna Hewitt
Production Manager: John Laister

Printed and bound in Singapore

THE BARNABAS
365
Story
Bible

STORIES BY

Sally Ann Wright

PICTURES BY

Honor Ayres

Paola Bertolini Grudina

Estelle Corke

Frank Endersby

Melanie Florian

Moira Maclean

Carla Manea

Krisztina Kállai Nagy

Martina Peluso

Heather Stuart

CONTENTS

1
In the very beginning
Genesis 1:1–5

In the very beginning, there was no earth or sky, trees or flowers, animals or people. There was nothing at all. Everything was quiet and dark. Then God said, 'Let there be light!' A beautiful warm glow broke through the darkness and there was light. 'That's good!' God said to himself. God called the light 'day' and the darkness 'night'.

So now there was light where before there was only darkness and there were blue skies where before there was only water.

2
God makes the sky
Genesis 1:6–8

God said, 'Let there be a big, wide, beautiful space.' God created a big, blue space above the dark waters below. God called the space 'sky'.

3
God fills the land
Genesis 1:9–13

Then God said, 'Let the waters be gathered together so that there will be some dry places.' And when God spoke, it happened, so that now there were dry places as well as watery places. God called the dry places 'land' and the watery places 'seas'. And God saw that what he had created was good. 'Now let the land be filled with good things that grow—leafy trees and flowering

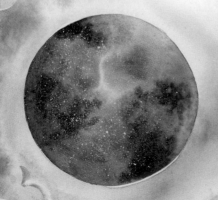

plants with fruits and seeds.' And so the land produced all kinds of vegetation. So now there was light where before there was darkness and blue skies where there was water; there was land and sea and shape and colour with all the plants and trees, fruit, flowers and vegetables. And God saw that what he had created was good.

4
God orders the heavens
Genesis 1:14–19

Then God said, 'Let there be lights in the sky to divide the day from the night and the times and the seasons upon the earth.' And when God spoke, it happened, so that now the sky was scattered with stars. The sun gave warmth to the days and the bright moon brought light to the dark night sky. So now there was light where before there was darkness and blue skies where there was water; there was land and sea and shape and colour with all the plants and trees, fruit, flowers and vegetables; there were sun, moon, stars and planets, night and day. And God saw that what he had created was good.

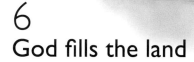

5
God fills the sea and the sky

Genesis 1:20–23

Then God said, 'Let the sea be filled with all kinds of living creatures and the sky with birds of every kind.' So God made the creatures that crawled along the sea bed and those with fins and tails to dart and swim in the waters. God made the winged birds that called and cooed and sang. He blessed them all so that they would increase in number. Now there was light and blue skies; land and sea and shape and colour; sun, moon, stars and planets; there were fish and birds that swam in the sea and flew in the sky. And God saw that what he had created was good.

6
God fills the land

Genesis 1:24–25

Then God said, 'Let the land be filled with all kinds of animals.' So God made creatures large and small, striped, spotted, plain and patterned; soft and furry, hard and spiky. Some moved on the ground and others climbed trees. And God saw that what he had created was good.

8
God rests
Genesis 2:1–3

When God had finished making his world and all the wonderful things in it, he listened to the sound of the birds singing and saw the sunlight filtering through the leafy trees. He watched the animals coming to drink water in the brooks and streams. He smelled the flowering plants and heard the buzz of many busy bees. God saw that it was not only good, it was very good. Then God rested. His work was done.

7
God makes people
Genesis 1:26–31

God's world was full of sound and colour and variety. But God had not finished yet. God made people who were more like him—able to think and feel and love. He made them male and female, man and woman, to be his friends. God gave them his world to look after from the fish and birds to every creepy crawly thing that lived on the earth.

9
The garden of Eden
Genesis 2:8–17

God gave Adam and Eve—the man
and the woman he had made—a
beautiful place to live in. It was called
the garden of Eden. There was a
clear stream with cool water to
drink, trees full of delicious fruits
to eat and everything that they
needed. Adam gave names to all the
animals and together Adam and Eve
tended the garden. God told them
they could eat from every tree there
except the one in the middle of the
garden, the tree of the knowledge
of good and evil. So the people lived
there happily with God as their
friend.

10
The first temptation
Genesis 3:1–5

One day, a serpent came to Eve with
a whispery voice. 'Did God tell you
not to eat the fruit from the trees
in the garden?' he said. 'No, God
said we can eat from every tree
except from the tree in the middle
of the garden,' she replied. 'But do
you know why he said this?' said
the serpent again. 'God knows
that if you eat from this tree, you
will become as clever as he is. You
will know all that God knows.
Why don't you try it and see what
happens? Why don't you just try it
and see…?'

11
The first sin
Genesis 2:6–8

Eve looked at the ripe fruit and saw
that it was very beautiful. It looked
especially juicy. And Eve liked the
idea of being wise and knowing as

much as God did. She looked back at the serpent, considering what to do. Then Eve reached up and picked a piece of the fruit. She took a bite. Then she shared some with Adam. Suddenly they were afraid. Up until that moment they had known only happiness, only good things. But now they realised that what they had done was wrong. They were ashamed, they felt guilty. When they heard God coming to talk to them in the evening, Adam and Eve hid from him. They knew they had disobeyed God.

12
Shame and punishment
Genesis 2:9–24

'Where are you?' God called to his friends. 'Why are you hiding?' Adam told God that they were afraid, they felt ashamed… 'It's Eve's fault,' said Adam. 'She gave me the fruit—I only ate it.' Then Eve said, 'It's not my fault; it's the serpent's—he tempted me and I picked it!' Then God spoke to the people he had made. 'Now you know the difference between what is good and what is bad, what is right and what is wrong. You have not trusted me to take care of you. Now you must live by the choices you have made.'

13
Cain and Abel
Genesis 4:1–2

Some time later, Eve became pregnant. She gave birth to her first child, a son. They called him Cain. Eve knew that God had blessed her, even though Adam and Eve no longer knew God as their friend. Eve became pregnant again and gave birth to a second son. They called him Abel. Cain grew up to be a farmer, working in the fields to grow food. Abel grew up to be a shepherd and he raised flocks of sheep and goats.

14
Gifts for God
Genesis 4:3–5; Hebrews 11:4

When Cain and Abel had good harvests and many new-born lambs and kids, they wanted to thank

God for taking care of them. Abel chose his best lamb and gave it to God to say thank you. Cain gave some of his grain. God was pleased with Abel's gift because he knew that Abel had come with faith and thanksgiving in his heart. But God knew that Cain had given his gift because he thought he had to. Cain didn't really care about God.

15
Cain's jealous nature
Genesis 4:5–12, 25

Cain knew that God was not pleased with him. Cain knew that God was pleased with his younger brother. Cain was angry and jealous. He sulked. 'Be careful, Cain,' said God. 'You should not be angry—if you do what is right, there is no need to be unhappy. But if you let your anger control you, you will regret it.' Cain did not listen to God. Instead he plotted and schemed. 'Let's go for a walk together,' he suggested to Abel. Then while they were out walking, Cain attacked and killed his younger brother. 'Where is your brother, Cain?' God asked. 'How do I know? Am I his keeper?' Cain asked. But God already knew what Cain had done. 'You have done a terrible thing,' God said. 'You will never be able to forget that you have taken a life.' Adam and Eve had lost a son but later God blessed them with another. His name was Seth.

16
A good man called Noah
Genesis 6:5–10

After some time, God's world had many people living in it. But it was no longer the perfect place that God had intended it to be. God looked with great sadness at the way people told lies and cheated and stole from each other. They fought and killed each other. God had made people to be his friends but no one remembered who he was; no one, that is, except Noah.

17
A huge building plan
Genesis 6:9–10, 14–21

Noah had a wife and three sons who were grown up and married. Unlike the people around him, Noah was good and kind. So when God spoke to Noah, Noah heard him. Noah listened. 'The world is full of violence and cruelty,' God said. 'It cannot go on like this. We must start again.' God told Noah that soon

there would be a great flood that would cover the land. Everything would be destroyed. 'You must build a huge boat, an ark,' God told Noah.

'I will give you instructions for exactly how big it must be and how it should be built. Then you need to collect two each of every animal that I have made so they will be kept safe until after the flood.'

18
Noah's ark
Genesis 6:22

Noah was no longer a young man but he trusted God. His neighbours laughed when they saw him felling cypress trees and cutting them into logs. They made fun of him when they saw the shape of a boat being formed. Surely Noah was a crazy old man! But Noah and his family sawed and hammered and worked hard building the ark, just as God had told them to, until one day, it was ready. The ark was huge—longer than a football field and higher than a three-storey building!

was room on board for them all. It took seven days. And when the last one was on the ark, the rain began to fall.

20
40 days and 40 nights
Genesis 7:11–12

The rain fell, hour after hour, day after day, for 40 days and 40 nights. Pitter, patter, drip, drop, splish, splash. The streams became rivers and the rivers became seas. The houses were covered, the treetops were covered and the mountains were covered. And the ark rose steadily on the floodwaters till there

19
Animals come to Noah
Genesis 7:6–10

Noah and his family watched as, two by two, animals of every kind came when the ark was ready. Elephants and tigers, flamingoes and giraffes, rabbits and foxes, all climbed on board the ark that Noah had built. There were male and female of each one—and God had made sure there

was nothing to be seen but water, water everywhere around them. Noah and his wife and his sons and their wives spent day after day feeding the animals and clearing up after them. They all listened to the rain drumming on the roof and wondered when the rain would stop.

21
The raven goes free
Genesis 8:1–7

Then one day, they all looked at each other and listened. What could they hear? What was different? Silence. The rain had stopped. Noah watched and waited and waited and watched. A wind was blowing. The sky was

clearing. Slowly, very slowly, the waters were going down. Soon they could see the tops of the mountains and the ark came to rest on Mount Ararat. Noah watched and waited and waited and watched a little longer, a

little longer... Then one day he set free a raven to see if it was time to leave the ark. The raven stretched its wings wide and flew away.

22
The dove and the olive leaf
Genesis 8:8–12

Then Noah sent out a dove. It flapped its wings gently through the blue sky, looking for a place to rest its feet. But the dove soon returned—water still covered the earth. Noah brought the dove back inside the ark for another seven days. Then he sent it out once more. This time the dove returned to him in the evening carrying a fresh green olive leaf in its beak! Now Noah knew that the water had gone down below the level of the trees and the leaves were sprouting again. Noah waited another seven days, then he set the dove free. This time it did not return.

23
A brand-new world
Genesis 8:15–22

Finally God told Noah it was safe to open the door and set all the animals free to roam the earth once more. 'Now they can increase and grow again in numbers,' said God. So Noah brought his family out of the ark and all the animals streamed out too, one kind after another, two by two. The earth was dry now and clean and new. Noah made an altar to God to thank him for keeping them all safe from the flood.

24
A beautiful rainbow
Genesis 9:8–17

Noah looked up in the sky and saw that God had made a beautiful rainbow appear. 'The people I have

made are not perfect,' said God. 'But I will never destroy the earth and all the people and creatures on it by flood again. Go now and have children so that there will again be many people who live on the earth.

And whenever you see a rainbow, remember my promise that the earth will never again be destroyed by flood.'

21

25
God chooses Abraham

Genesis 12:1–4

A long time after Noah, God spoke to a man named Abraham. 'It's time to move on,' God said. 'Pack up all your things and take your family and servants with you. I will tell you where to go.' Abraham and his wife Sarah were already old. They didn't know where they were going, and they didn't know how long it would take them, but they trusted God.

26
Abraham moves to Canaan

Genesis 12:5

Abraham had lots of sheep and goats and cattle. He gathered up the tents where he lived, and all the things he owned and went with his wife, Sarah, his nephew, Lot, his servants and all of his animals… far away from his home and across the hot, dusty desert. They stopped and made camp many times on their long journey until they arrived in a land

27
A very special blessing
Genesis 12:7

The land of Canaan was made green by water. Everywhere trees and plants were growing. There would be plenty of food for Abraham's animals. It was a good place to be. 'Now I will bless you, Abraham,' God said. 'This land will belong to your children and your children's children.' Abraham loved God and he trusted him but he couldn't help wondering how that could happen when they didn't have even one tiny baby of their own.

called Canaan. Then Abraham looked around him at the place that God had given him as his new home. It was beautiful.

28
Too many animals!

Genesis 13:5–9

Time passed and still Abraham
and Sarah had no baby to love
and take care of. But Abraham's
sheep had baby sheep. His goats
had baby goats. God blessed both

Abraham and Lot so much that they
couldn't move for animals! 'Choose
anywhere you would like to live,
Lot,' Abraham told his nephew. 'We'll
share this land between us so there
is room for us all to be happy.'

29
A new home for Lot

Genesis 13:10–13

Lot chose the land to the east, a
beautiful green valley, watered by
the River Jordan. He made his home
near a place called Sodom, close to

another city called Gomorrah. But Lot did not have good neighbours. Both cities were well known for the bad people who lived there and did bad, cruel things. So while Lot lived among bad people, Abraham stayed in Canaan and was happy.

30
Visitors for Abraham
Genesis 18:1–10

Abraham was resting in the shade in the heat of the day when he thought he saw men—three men— walking towards him. Abraham got to his feet and went to greet them. He offered them somewhere to rest and then set about preparing

food for them to eat. Soon Abraham realised that God had sent them with a very special message for him. 'Get ready for a wonderful surprise,' they said. 'By this time next year, Sarah will be nursing your baby son!' Sarah was listening from inside her tent. She laughed quietly to herself. Surely she was far too old to have a baby now?

31
Ten good men
Genesis 18:17–33

God had heard about the bad things that were happening in Sodom and Gomorrah. The men who had come to see Abraham had also come with a mission to see if the people were as bad as everyone said. If they were, the cities would be destroyed. Abraham knew that God was good and kind. So he asked, 'Will you spare the cities if only 50 good

people live there?' God said, 'No, I will spare them.' So Abraham asked again, 'What if there are 45 good people?' God said, 'I will spare them.'

Abraham dared to ask again… and again… and again. Finally Abraham asked, 'Please, Lord, will you spare the cities if only ten good people live there?' God promised that he would not destroy them for the sake of just ten good people.

32
Sodom and Gomorrah
Genesis 19:1–13

God sent two angels to see if there were any good people in Sodom and Gomorrah. Lot still lived there with his wife and daughters. Lot came to meet them and welcomed them at the gate of the city. 'Come to my home and rest,' said Lot. 'Let me prepare food for you.' But when the people of the city found out that Lot had strangers in his home, they hammered on his door. They demanded that Lot send them out. Lot stood in the doorway to protect his visitors but the men outside were fierce and angry. The angels pulled Lot back inside the house.

33
The angels' warning
Genesis 19:14–25

Lot was a good man. The angels warned him to take his family and any friends he had and run as far away as possible. The city would be destroyed by the morning. But only his wife and daughters would go with Lot; only four people escaped that night. 'Don't look back!' the angels called after them.

terrible sound as fire and brimstone rained down on the cities of Sodom and Gomorrah. Everything there was destroyed. Lot's wife forgot the angels' warning and she looked back—only to be turned into a pillar of salt. Only Lot and his daughters were saved.

34
The pillar of salt
Genesis 19:26

Lot and his family ran until they could run no more. They heard the

35
God keeps his promises
Genesis 21:1–8

Abraham knew that God had kept his promise about Sodom and Gomorrah. He also knew that God had kept his promise about a baby for Sarah! Abraham was going to be a father at last. It was a miracle. Abraham was as impatient as Sarah to hold his little baby son in his arms. 'God has made me so happy!'

said Sarah when her son was born. They named their baby Isaac which means laughter, because Sarah had laughed when she was told she would have a baby.

36
Abraham's faith
Genesis 22:1–8

Abraham loved and trusted God. He also loved his son Isaac very much. So when God asked Abraham to do something very hard indeed,

Abraham was very sad. Isaac had grown into a fine boy. Now God was asking Abraham to trust him with the son he loved more than anything. Abraham took Isaac with him up the mountain with a heavy heart.

37
A very hard test
Genesis 22:9–12

Isaac was happy to be with his father. He walked beside him trying to keep up. 'We're going to show God how much we love him,' Abraham told his son. Then Isaac asked, 'We have the wood for the sacrifice, but where is the lamb?' 'Don't worry,' said Abraham sadly. 'God will provide the sacrifice.'

38
God's blessing
Genesis 22:13–18

Abraham got everything ready for the sacrifice and took the knife in his hand. But before he had time to use it, an angel stopped him.

Abraham put down the knife and hugged his son very, very tightly. 'Now I know how much you love me,' said God. 'I know you trust me even when it is very hard. I will bless you, now and always.' Then Abraham saw a ram caught in a bush. He sacrificed the animal instead.

be Isaac's wife. When the servant arrived at the place where Abraham's family still lived, it was very hot and he was tired and thirsty. He sat down and prayed for God's help. 'Please help me to find a girl for Isaac—someone kind enough to offer me water to drink on this hot day—and then water my ten camels too.'

39
A good, kind woman
Genesis 24:1–14

When Isaac was grown up, Sarah died. Abraham was old too and he was afraid that his son was lonely. He wanted to find for him a wife from his own family rather than from the people who lived nearby. So Abraham sent his servant on a long journey to find a good, kind woman who would be happy to

40
The girl at the well
Genesis 24:15–27

While the servant waited, he saw a beautiful girl come towards the well. She smiled at him. 'May I have a drink?' the servant asked her. 'Of course!' she answered. She drew the water from the well and offered it to him. Then the girl added, 'Let me bring some water for your camels too. They must be so thirsty!" The servant silently thanked God. He knew that God had answered his prayer. He discovered that the girl was called Rebekah and that she was the granddaughter of Abraham's brother. Rebekah took the servant back to meet her family. They listened to his story and knew that God had led him there. They were happy that Rebekah should return with him to marry Isaac. The servant stayed with them that night and then took Rebekah home with him.

41
Abraham's growing family
Genesis 25:20–25

Isaac was watching and waiting for the return of his father's servant. When he met Rebekah, he was happy that she wanted to be his wife. Some time later, Rebekah gave birth to twin sons—two little boys who would grow up to lead two separate nations. They were called Esau and Jacob.

42
Isaac's favourite
Genesis 25:26–28

Esau was born first. Even as a baby, he was already strong and healthy, with lots of red hair. He grew up to be a skilful hunter and he loved the outdoor life. Isaac was proud of his eldest son. He liked spending time with Esau best of all, looking after their many sheep and goats.

43
Rebekah's favourite
Genesis 25:26–29

Jacob was born second, but he was born holding on to Esau's heel. The two boys were different in looks and character. Jacob grew up to be a quiet boy. He didn't like hunting and preferred to spend time with his mother. Jacob was dark in colouring and had smooth skin. He was Rebekah's favourite. Esau would often come back from a day's hunting to smell something good simmering in a pot. Jacob was a good cook.

44
A bowl of spicy stew
Genesis 25:29–34

One day, Esau returned to his father's tents hot and tired and hungry. He found Jacob and could smell the spicy lentil stew he was

cooking. 'Mmmm, that smells delicious,' Esau said. 'I'm so hungry, I could die!' Jacob was quiet but he was clever. He kept stirring the stew as he thought quickly. 'You can have some now,' he replied, 'as long as you will trade it for father's blessing.' Jacob knew that only the older son was allowed that special blessing which was given before the father died. 'You can have anything you want if I can eat that stew!' replied Esau. So Jacob gave his brother a bowl of the tasty food and watched him eat hungrily. Esau had sold his birthright to Jacob for a bowl of spicy stew. He had given away a very special blessing and he didn't seem to care.

45
Isaac's last wish
Genesis 27:1–4

Isaac grew to be an old man. His
back became stooped. He couldn't
go for long walks any more. Soon
he began to lose his sight. He found
that he couldn't see very well at all.
He called Esau to his tent one day.
'My son, I know it will not be long
before I die. I want to give you my
blessing. But first—go and hunt for
me with your bow and arrow. Bring
home something tasty and cook me
my favourite meal.' Isaac didn't know
anything about Esau's trade with his
younger brother years before.

46
Rebekah's idea
Genesis 27:5–17

Rebekah had heard all that Isaac said.
She had another idea. Jacob was
her favourite son; Rebekah wanted
Jacob to have the blessing instead.
So while Esau was out hunting,
Rebekah started to cook a tasty meal
for Isaac. She then called Jacob and
told him to dress in some
of Esau's clothes so that he
would smell like his brother.
She covered his neck and
arms in goatskin so he would
feel hairy like his brother. Now
everything was ready: Jacob could
go to see his father and make him
believe that he was blessing Esau…

47
Isaac gives his blessing
Genesis 27:18–29

Isaac heard someone come into his tent. 'Is that you already, Esau?' he asked his younger son. 'God must have blessed you to have such a good day's hunting.' Then Isaac touched his son and felt his hairy skin; he smelled the clothes that he wore. Isaac was satisfied. He ate the meal that Rebekah had made for him and blessed Jacob. 'May God bless you now and always. You will become a rich man and will rule over your brother.'

48
Esau returns
Genesis 27:30–46

Not long afterwards, Esau returned
from his hunting trip. He prepared
the food to take to his father and
carried it in to his tent. 'I have come
for your blessing, Father,' he said.
Then Isaac knew that he had been
tricked and Esau realised that he
was too late. They were both angry.
'I'm going to kill my little brother
for this!' Esau said and went looking
for Jacob. Rebekah saw that the
brothers could not live together
happily now. 'Go, Jacob,' she said to
her youngest son. 'Go and stay with
your Uncle Laban for a while. You
will be safe there.'

49
Jacob's dream
Genesis 28:10–22

Jacob set off on his journey, sad to
leave his home. When night came,
Jacob made camp under the stars
with a rock for his pillow. While

he slept, Jacob had some strange dreams. He dreamed of a ladder leading up to heaven, to the very throne of God, with angels climbing up and down. Then Jacob heard God's voice. 'I am the God who promised to take care of your father and your grandfather,' said God. 'Now I will take care of you. I will give the land where you are sleeping to you and to your descendants. I will be your God, too.' So Jacob woke up next morning knowing that he was blessed by his father and by God himself.

50
Cousin Rachel
Genesis 29:1–20

When Jacob was not far from Haran where his uncle lived, he stopped by a well. There he met a beautiful shepherdess

called Rachel. He found out that Rachel was his cousin, Laban's daughter, and soon Jacob was being welcomed into their family. Jacob worked hard for Laban, taking care of his sheep and goats. 'How can I reward you for all you have done?' Laban asked Jacob. Jacob knew immediately what his answer should be—he had fallen in love with Rachel. 'I will work for you for seven years if you will let me marry Rachel,' Jacob told him. Laban agreed. Jacob was strong and useful to him.

had tricked him! The woman under the veil was not Rachel but her older sister, Leah! 'It's our custom that the older sister gets married first,' Laban explained. Now Jacob knew that Laban was not an honest man.

51

Jacob is married…

Genesis 29:21–27

Jacob was happy to work hard for his uncle. Every day brought him nearer to the time when he could marry Rachel. But seven years later, when Jacob went to kiss his new wife, he found that his uncle Laban

52

Jacob is married again!

Genesis 29:27–28

Jacob was very sad that Rachel was not his wife. But Laban told Jacob that as long as he worked for him for another seven years, he could marry Rachel, too. So, since many

people had more than one wife at that time, Jacob married Rachel. Now he had two wives. Rachel was very happy but Leah was not quite so happy. She knew that Jacob did not love her as much as he loved Rachel.

53
Jacob's many children
Genesis 29:31–35

God blessed Leah with many children to love, but it was a long time before Rachel had babies of her own. Jacob's family grew so that he eventually had twelve sons and a daughter. They were called: Reuben, Simeon, Levi, Judah, Dan, Naphtali, Gad, Asher, Issachar, Zebulun, Dinah, Joseph and Benjamin. The last two sons were Rachel's children. And like his own mother and father, Jacob had a favourite. He loved Joseph most of all.

54
Laban's clever trick
Genesis 30:25–36

Jacob had been living with his uncle for a long time. The time came when he decided he wanted to go home. Laban didn't want Jacob to leave. It wasn't only that he would miss his daughters and his grandchildren— Laban knew that God had blessed him while Jacob had been there. He was afraid of what would happen when he went away. 'Of course you must go home,' Laban lied, 'but wait until you have built up a herd of speckled or spotted animals.' Then Laban hid them all.

55
Spots and speckles
Genesis 30:37–43

Jacob knew he couldn't trust his uncle any more. So he had a plan of his own. Jacob found a way to breed the sheep and goats secretly so that soon, everywhere he looked, the animals were black and white and every variation of spotted and speckled! When his herd was big and strong, Jacob gathered his wives and children and all his animals—and crept away, without telling his uncle. Jacob started on the long journey back to Canaan.

56
A new name for Jacob
Genesis 32:24–32

Jacob knew that God had blessed him as he had once promised. But he had left home because he had made his brother angry. He was worried about what would happen when he met Esau again. One night, he was sitting alone by a river when a stranger came and attacked him in the darkness. They struggled all night, wrestling with each other. When the sun rose, Jacob realised that the stranger had not been a man but an angel sent by God. 'From now on your name will be Israel,' said the angel. 'God has special plans for you.' After this, Jacob's children came to be known as the Israelites.

57
Friends and brothers
Genesis 33:1–17

That day, Jacob was very worried when he saw that his brother had come out to meet him with 400 men! Jacob told his family to wait in safety while he went on alone to meet Esau and his army. Jacob could hardly believe his eyes when he saw Esau smiling and coming forward to hug him. Esau had forgiven Jacob long ago. Now they were not just brothers but friends. God really had blessed Jacob.

58
Joseph, the favourite son
Genesis 37:3–4

Joseph knew that he was Jacob's favourite son. His brothers knew it too. One day Jacob made a present of a beautiful long sleeved coat to Joseph. Joseph felt very special. His brothers looked at each other. They were not happy. It was hard to know that your father did not treat you all fairly.

59
Joseph, the dreamer
Genesis 37:5–8

One night, Joseph dreamed. He had such a strange dream that he told his brothers about it the next morning. 'Listen to this,' he said.

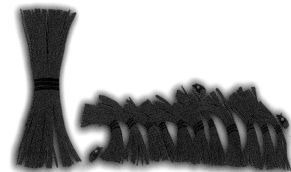

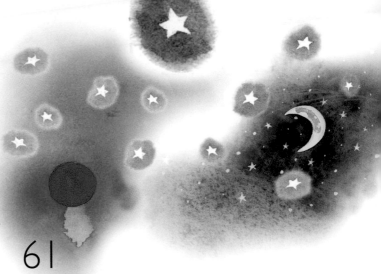

'I dreamed that we were all tying bundles of grain. Then my bundle stood up very straight while yours all bowed down in front of mine!' The brothers looked angrily at each other again. Did it mean something? Would Joseph one day rule over his brothers like a king?

60
Very angry brothers
Genesis 37:9–11

Then Joseph dreamed again. This time he dreamed that the sun, the moon and eleven stars bowed down to him. When he told his family this they were sure the meaning was clear. One day the whole family would bow down before Joseph. Jacob wondered what the future would hold for Joseph; but his brothers began to think of ways to make sure that Joseph would not be telling them his dreams for much longer…

61
Joseph, far from home
Genesis 37:12–19

Joseph's brothers were often far from home, watching over their father's sheep in distant fields. One day, Jacob decided to send Joseph to see how they were. Joseph went to the fields near Shechem where they were supposed to be but he couldn't find them there. He asked someone if he knew where his brothers were and was told that they had moved on with the sheep to another place. So Joseph walked on in search of his brothers. When he was still a long way off, they saw him coming. 'Look who's coming!' they said to each other. 'Here comes that dreamer!'

62
A very cruel plot
Genesis 37:20–24

As Joseph came closer, his brothers talked about him. 'How can we get rid of Joseph?' they said. 'We should make sure he can't be a problem to us any more!' They were not just jealous of Joseph—they hated him! 'Let's kill him!' said one. 'We could tell our father that he has been eaten by a wild animal!' When everyone agreed, Reuben, the oldest brother, stopped them. 'Let's throw him into this dry well for a while,' he suggested. Reuben secretly planned to rescue him later. So when Joseph came to greet them, his brothers tore off his special coat and put him in a deep, dark hole.

63
20 silver coins
Genesis 37:25–28

The brothers settled down to eat their lunch while Joseph, confused and frightened, shouted for help from the deep hole in the ground. Then the brothers saw some spice traders on camels approaching. 'I have a better idea about Joseph...' said Judah. Soon the brothers had 20 silver coins chinking in their hands— they had sold him as a slave and Joseph was on his way to Egypt. The brothers told Jacob that Joseph had been killed by a wild animal. Jacob felt as if the world had ended when he lost his favourite son.

64
Potiphar's house
Genesis 39:1–7

Joseph thought about what had happened on the long, dusty journey to Egypt. He understood only one thing—that his brothers hated him. But God had not forgotten Joseph. He was sold as a slave to Potiphar, who was a kind master. Joseph worked very hard and proved to be good at everything he did. Soon Potiphar trusted Joseph with everything in his house. God blessed Potiphar because Joseph was there.

65
Things go badly wrong
Genesis 39:7–20

Joseph was a handsome young man; Potiphar's wife liked him very much. Every day she would try to kiss him—and every day, Joseph would try to get away from her! One day Potiphar's wife was so angry with Joseph that she told her husband lies about him—and Potiphar sent Joseph to prison. How had all this happened? How had everything gone so wrong?

45

66
The king's baker
Genesis 39:20–23; 40:16–18

Joseph worked hard in prison and God blessed him again. The guard trusted him; soon Joseph was his helper. One day, the king's baker and butler were thrown into prison too. Joseph listened as the baker told him about the dream he had dreamed the night before. The baker dreamed he had made three loaves of bread for the king, but the birds came along and ate them all. 'What can it mean?' the baker asked Joseph.

67
The king's butler
Genesis 40:1–23

The butler also had a strange dream. He dreamed that the king drank wine he had made from three branches of grapes. 'What can it mean?' he asked. God helped Joseph to understand both dreams. 'Don't worry!' Joseph told the butler. 'In three days, you will be out of prison and working once more for the king.' But there was bad news for the baker. 'I'm sorry,' said Joseph. 'In three days, you will be hanged…' And Joseph was right. When the butler left the prison, Joseph said, 'Don't forget me—tell the king I have done nothing wrong!'

68
The king's dream
Genesis 41:1–13

The butler DID forget Joseph until two years later when the king had strange dreams. He dreamed that seven fat, healthy cows were grazing by the Nile, when seven skinny, bony cows came up and ate them! Then he dreamed again, this time that seven thin parched ears of grain swallowed up seven plump golden ears of grain. 'What can it mean?' he asked all the wise men in his court. They looked at one another and they thought and they scratched their heads—but no one could tell the king the meaning of his dream. Then the butler dared to speak. 'Today, my King, I realise that two years ago I forgot something very important. I met a man, an innocent man, who was locked up in your prison. This man knows how to understand the meaning of dreams. Perhaps he can help you.'

69
Joseph is set free
Genesis 41:14–36

Joseph had been in prison now for years. He had almost given up hope of being free when he was brought from the prison and washed and shaved and made presentable to stand before the king of Egypt. When the king explained to Joseph that he needed someone who could explain his strange dreams, Joseph answered, 'I cannot explain your dreams, but my God knows everything. He will help you.' So the king explained to Joseph the two dreams he had had. Joseph listened and then he told the king what his dreams meant. 'Your dreams are both the same,' he said. 'God is sending you a warning. Soon we will have seven years with wonderful harvests; but it will be followed by seven years when nothing grows at all. There will be a terrible famine. What you need is someone to store enough grain in the first seven years so that no one will go hungry when the famine comes.'

70
Joseph's chain of office
Genesis 41:37–49

The king looked thoughtfully at Joseph and then at his wise men. 'Surely this is the man we should choose!' he said. 'God has told you what will happen—you are the man who will take charge of all the grain. Everyone will take orders from you.' Then he placed a ring on Joseph's hand, gave him fine clothes to wear and put a gold chain around his neck.

71
Feast and famine
Genesis 41:53–57

The good harvests came to Egypt, followed by the famine, just as Joseph had said. The people of Egypt cried out to the king for help in their hunger, and he said, 'Go to Joseph.' Once a slave, Joseph had become the most important man in Egypt apart from the king himself. Joseph opened the storehouses of grain and made sure everyone had enough to eat.

'You older boys must go to Egypt and buy food for us all so we can live.' So ten of Joseph's brothers went to Egypt, following the trail that Joseph had made many years before. Only Benjamin, Jacob's youngest son, stayed at home with his father.

72
Jacob and his sons
Genesis 42:1–3

The famine was not just in Egypt but also in Israel where Jacob and his family still lived. They heard that there was food in Egypt. 'You are hungry, I am hungry,' Jacob said.

73
Dreams come true
Genesis 42:5–10

When Joseph's brothers bowed low before the second most powerful person in all the land of Egypt, they did not recognise the man with the

ring on his hand and the gold chain around his neck as the boy they had known with the coloured coat. But Joseph recognised his brothers. 'We are your humble servants,' they said. 'We are hungry and have come to buy food.' It was as if Joseph's dreams had come true. Were Joseph's brothers the same men who had wanted to kill him; who had sold him to be a slave for 20 silver coins?

asked them about their family and said he wanted to meet their younger brother. Then he let them buy lots of grain and sent them home again. But before they left, Joseph hid the money they had paid in their sacks. He made one brother stay behind in Egypt so they would come back with their youngest brother, Benjamin. And then... Joseph waited until they were hungry once more.

74
Grain for Jacob's family
Genesis 42:11–38

Joseph did not tell his brothers who he was—he pretended he did not understand their strange language. 'Perhaps you are spies?' he said. He

75
Benjamin goes to Egypt
Genesis 43:1–34

Jacob was very upset that one of his sons had stayed in Egypt. And he did not understand why his money had been returned. And when the grain ran out, he did not want all his sons to go back to Egypt! But he had no choice. They would die without food. So he let Benjamin go back with them.

76
The silver cup
Genesis 44:1–34

Joseph was overjoyed to see his younger brother but still he did not tell them who he was. This time, Joseph put a silver cup into Benjamin's sack of grain so it looked as if he were a thief! Would his brothers defend Benjamin? Or would they leave him behind? The brothers were ready to go home when Joseph's servant shouted, 'STOP! Someone has stolen my master's silver cup!' Ten sacks were all searched and nothing was found. Then they looked in Benjamin's sack—and there was the missing cup! The brothers wept. 'Please! Punish me, not Benjamin!' they said. 'It will break our father's heart if he does not return!'

77
God's plan
Genesis 45:1–15

Joseph now knew all that he wanted to know about his brothers. He knew they were not the same men who had sold him as a slave. They had learned to be sorry and were kinder men. Joseph forgave them all that had happened. 'Look!' he told them. 'I am Joseph, your brother. You meant to harm me, but it was God's plan all along to bring me to Egypt. It has saved our family from hunger in the famine.' Then Joseph hugged his brothers. They were friends for the first time.

hardly believe his ears. But soon he was on his way there to see Joseph.

78
A gift from the king
Genesis 45:16–28; 46:1–4

When the king heard that Joseph's brothers had come to see him, he was pleased. 'Send them back to Canaan with as much food as they can carry!' he said. 'Then let them bring back your father and all the people in your family. I will give you the best land in Egypt where you can make your home with them.' So Joseph sent his brothers away with many good things as gifts for his father. 'Don't quarrel with each other on the journey!' he joked. When Jacob was told that his lost son was living in Egypt, he could

79
Fathers and sons
Genesis 46:1–7, 28–30

Then God spoke to Jacob. 'Don't be afraid to make your home in Egypt,' God said. 'I will go there with you and I will bring you back. Joseph will be there with you when you die.' Jacob took with him all his sons and their wives and children, all the aunts and uncles and cousins... When he met Joseph again they threw their arms around each other and cried with joy. Now they were all together again— one big happy family.

80
'God saved us all'
Genesis 50:1–26

Jacob was a very old man. He blessed Joseph's sons, Manasseh and Ephraim, before he breathed his last breath. Joseph was very, very sad when his father died but he made sure that Jacob was buried in Canaan as he had wished. Joseph's brothers were worried that Joseph would be cruel to them after his father's death but Joseph was kind. 'Don't be afraid,' Joseph said. 'God has saved us all by bringing us here, and I will make sure that no harm comes to you in Egypt.' Joseph himself lived long enough to see his great-great-grandchildren born. God had blessed him and all the children of Israel while they lived in Egypt. Before he died, Joseph told his brothers that God would take them back to the land of Canaan, the promised land, one day.

81
A cruel Egyptian king
Exodus 1:1–22

One day there was a new king who did not know what Joseph had done for Egypt. He only saw that the Israelites had grown to be too many people—and he was afraid. The king made them all his slaves. He made them work hard and he beat them.

But still they grew stronger. So the king ordered his soldiers to throw every newborn baby boy born to the Israelites into the River Nile...

82
Miriam's baby brother
Exodus 2:1–3

Miriam's mother had just had a baby son. They hid him from the soldiers for as long as they could but when he got to be bigger and cried even more loudly, Miriam's mother had to think of another plan. She made a waterproof woven basket and placed him inside. Then she hid it beside the River Nile, and told Miriam to watch and wait.

83
The princess and the baby
Exodus 2:2–6

Soon Miriam saw one of the king's daughters come to the river to have a bath. The princess heard the baby

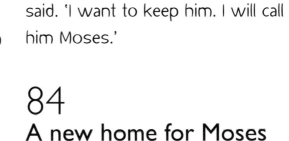

crying and asked her maid to fetch the basket. 'Poor little baby,' she said. 'I want to keep him. I will call him Moses.'

84
A new home for Moses
Exodus 2:7–9

Miriam popped up out of her hiding place. 'Shall I find an Israelite woman to take care of the little baby?' she asked. The princess agreed, and Miriam ran home to get her mother—the baby's mother! Moses then lived safely with his family until he was old enough to live in the palace with the princess.

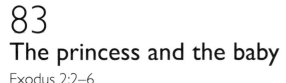

85
Moses kills a man
Exodus 2:10–14

Moses grew up in the king's palace and was educated in the way of the Egyptian boys. But he knew he was an Israelite. He could not help seeing what was happening to his people. It made Moses angry to see how badly they were being treated. Then one day, Moses saw an Israelite slave being beaten cruelly. He looked around to see if anyone was watching—and then he went out and killed the Egyptian slave driver. Moses was so afraid that the king would find out that he ran away.

86
A wife for Moses
Exodus 2:15–25

Moses went into the desert. After a while he met seven young women, all sisters, who were fetching water from a well. When Moses helped them, their father was grateful. Soon they were friends and he asked Moses if he would like to marry one of his daughters. So it was that Moses married and started a new life as a husband and a shepherd, working for his father-in-law. He lived with his new family in the desert for over 40 years.

87
The burning bush
Exodus 3:1–10

One day, while Moses was watching his sheep, he thought he saw a bush in the desert that seemed to be on fire. When he went closer, he saw that the leaves were not burning up. Then Moses heard the voice of God speaking to him from the flames. 'Moses! My people need you. They call out to me from their slavery. I want you to go to see the king of Egypt. Tell him that he must set my people free.'

91
Frogs, frogs and more frogs!

Exodus 8:1–15

When the people could not draw clean water from the River Nile, the king realised he had to agree.

But as soon as God took the blood red water away, the king changed his mind. Then God sent a second plague. 'Ribbit! Ribbit!' All over the land of Egypt, loud croaking noises could be heard. There were frogs in the houses, frogs in the beds, frogs in the cooking bowls—there were frogs everywhere! Then Moses and Aaron went again to the king of

Egypt. 'God says, "Let my people go!"' At first the king said, 'Yes!' but when God took the frogs away, the king changed his mind.

92
A cloud of biting gnats
Exodus 8:16–19

God sent a third plague on the land of Egypt. The people watched as the dust of the earth seemed to gather into a big cloud. Then the air was filled with tiny biting gnats. Zzz! Phhttt! The people of Egypt and their animals were attacked by the buzzing creatures that left them bitten all over with sore, itchy bites. Moses and Aaron went again to the king of Egypt. 'God says, "Let my people go!"' At first the king said, 'Yes!' but when God took the gnats away, the king changed his mind.

93
A swarm of buzzing flies
Exodus 8:16–32

God sent a fourth plague on the land of Egypt. This time the people saw a swarm of flies coming towards them. Buzzzzzz! Buzzzzzz! The flies invaded the king's palace and the homes of all the people who worked for him. Swarms of flies covered the ground they walked on. It was horrible! But the flies did not go near God's people, the Israelites. Then Moses and Aaron went again to the king of Egypt. 'God says, "Let my people go!"' The king said 'Yes!' but when God took the flies away, the king changed his mind.

94
Dead and dying animals
Exodus 9:1–7

God sent a fifth plague on the land of Egypt. Now the cows, sheep, horses, donkeys, camels and all the livestock out in the fields in the land of Egypt became ill and died. The king sent men to check on the animals belonging to the Israelites but not one of them had become ill. The animals of the Israelites had lived. Then Moses and Aaron went again to the king of Egypt. 'God says, "Let my people go!"' The king was very angry and he would not listen to the message that came from God.

95
Lumps, bumps and boils
Exodus 9:8–17

God sent a sixth plague on the land of Egypt. How many chances did God have to give the king? Moses stood before the man in charge of all of Egypt and threw handfuls of soot up into the air as God had told him to do. Then the Egyptians began to break out

in boils. Red, itchy, swollen bumps popped up all over their skin so they were red-raw with scratching. Ouch! Moses and Aaron spoke to the king again. 'God says, "Let my people go!"' The king still would not listen to the message that came from God.

96
Thunder, hail and lightning
Exodus 9:18–35

God sent a seventh plague on the land of Egypt. He told Moses to go to the king and ask again to let the Israelites go. Then he was to give the king a warning. So Moses went with God's message to the king. 'God says that you must let

his people go; but if you do not, God, who is Lord of all the earth, will send a storm so terrible that everything and everyone in its path will be destroyed.' Some of the Egyptians believed God and brought everything they owned inside to escape the storm. But those who stayed outside were destroyed by terrible thunder, hail and lightning. The storm did not destroy the Israelites who were living in the land of Goshen. This time the king was sorry. 'Your God is in the right—I will let your people go,' he said.

97
The plague of locusts
Exodus 10:1–20

Moses went outside and held out his hands—and God stilled the raging storm. But as soon as the king saw that the thunder and hail and lightning had stopped, he changed his mind. He would not let the Israelites go. Then God sent the eighth plague on the land of Egypt. Now even the king's servants were begging him to listen to God. An east wind blew, and the next morning, locusts covered the land. They filled the fields and they filled the houses. They ate everything that the hail had not already destroyed. The land was stripped bare. Nothing green was left in Egypt. Nothing so terrible had ever been seen before. Once more the king asked Moses to take away the plague. But when God banished the locusts to the Red Sea, the king changed his mind.

98
Three days of darkness
Exodus 10:21–29

Then God sent the ninth plague on the land of Egypt. Moses stretched out his hand towards the sky and God brought darkness on the land for three whole days. Only in Goshen where the Israelites lived was there light. The king called for Moses and Aaron. 'Go—take your men, women and children with you.

But do not take your animals when you go.' But the Israelites needed their animals. So the king would not let them go. 'Get out!' he shouted. 'And don't come back! I never want to see you again.'

99
Weeping and wailing
Exodus 11:1–10

Now there could be no more chances for the king. God told Moses that just as the king had tried to destroy all the Israelite baby boys by drowning them in the River Nile, at midnight God would send the tenth plague. All the first-born males in Egypt—both animals and children—would die. Soon there would be much weeping and wailing in the land of Egypt.

100
The angel of death
Exodus 12:1–13

'Tell my people to get ready for a long journey,' God said to Moses. 'They must get ready all their animals and pack all their things together. They must eat a meal of roast lamb, bitter herbs and bread made without yeast, dressed and prepared to leave Egypt. They must mark their doorposts with the blood of the lamb. When I see this sign, the angel of death will pass over you.' God kept his promise.

101
The king says 'Go!'
Exodus 12:29–41

The last plague caused much sorrow for the people of Egypt. In every house the firstborn son died. When the king held his own son in his arms, he called for Moses and Aaron. 'Take your people and go!' he said. The Israelites were ready.

They gathered their families, all their possessions and the embalmed body of Joseph, and followed Moses out of Egypt.

102
God leads his people
Exodus 13:17–22

God had set his people free. But this was just the beginning. As they followed Moses out of the land where they had been slaves for so long, they wondered where they would go next. 'Trust God,' Moses told them. 'We are his people. He will lead the way.' And God did. God made a pillar of cloud for all the Israelites to follow during the day. Even the families who were far away, travelling at the back of the long trail of people, could see the cloud from far away. At night, God led them with a pillar of bright fire that shone in the darkness. They followed, trusting God to take them to a place where they could be safe.

103
The king changes his mind…
Exodus 14:1–12

The night had passed; days had followed; and the king of Egypt was angry. He realised that he had let his slaves go and he was not happy.

Once again, the king changed his mind. He made ready his army and all the chariots in Egypt and chased after the Israelites. They found them while they were beside the sea. The Israelites were trapped: the Red Sea was in front of them and the Egyptian army behind them. They were terrified.

104
Safe on the other side
Exodus 14:13–31

'Don't be afraid,' Moses told them. 'Trust God.' Then he held out his stick over the sea and it parted so the Israelites could walk safely across on a path through the sea. When the king's chariots tried to follow, Moses raised his stick again and a flood of water washed over the Egyptians. The Israelites were safe on the other side. They thanked God for saving them.

105
Walking without water

Exodus 15:22–27

The Israelites were happy to be free... but it was hot and dusty walking through the desert. They soon began to be tired and thirsty and grumpy. Moses told them to trust God. He had brought them across the Red Sea—he would not let them die of thirst. 'God will give us everything we need,' said Moses. And God did. God led them to an oasis with twelve fresh springs of water and palm trees with sweet dates to eat.

106
Food from heaven

Exodus 16:1–21

The Israelites were happy for a while... but it was not long before they were grumpy again. 'We were better off when we were slaves in Egypt!' they complained. 'At least we had good food to eat!' 'Trust God,' said Moses. 'God will give us everything we need.' And God did.

God blessed them by giving them quails to eat in the evenings and he rained down sweet bread from heaven each morning.

107
Laws on the mountain
Exodus 19:1–25

Day after day, month after month, the Israelites walked in the desert. They set up camp when they reached Mount Sinai. Then God told Moses that he would make the Israelites a special, holy people,

as long as they listened to him and obeyed his laws. The people promised they would do this. Moses told the people to wait for him while he went up the mountain to receive these laws from God. No one was to follow. The top of the mountain was covered in a thick cloud of smoke; the people could not see Moses and they could not see God. But they saw the flash of lightning and heard the sound of thunder

and a very loud trumpet. Then God gave Moses the laws that were to guide his people, rules written on two large stones. They were known for ever afterwards as the Ten Commandments.

108
Ten special rules
Exodus 21:2–26

The rules God gave the people were to help them to worship God and to live in peace with each other.

1. God is the only God. You should have no other in his place.
2. You should not make a god out of anything else on the earth. Worship only God.
3. Use God's name when you speak to God but do not misuse it because it is special and holy.
4. Keep the sabbath as a special holy day when you can worship God and rest from your work.
5. Love and respect your parents.
6. Don't murder anyone.
7. Don't steal someone else's wife or husband.
8. Don't steal anything from anyone.
9. Don't lie to anyone.
10. Don't be jealous of things that other people have.

109
Moses talks with God
Exodus 21—31

God explained all these laws to Moses. He helped him to understand that the way to live together happily and in peace was to act kindly and

justly and take care of those who could not help themselves. God asked Moses to explain these laws to the people.

110
The golden calf
Exodus 32:1–6

While Moses was on the mountain talking with God, the people waited below. They began to get anxious. He had been away for such a long time. So they went to Aaron and asked him to make them a god they could see, so they could worship it. Aaron remembered that the Egyptians had a god made in the shape of a calf. So he told them to bring all their rings and jewellery and made them into a golden calf.

111
Moses prays for the people
Exodus 32:7–35

God saw the golden calf. When Moses saw it he could not believe that they had promised to love only God—and already broken that law. 'Forgive them,' Moses prayed to God. 'They are weak. They need to learn to trust you. Remember that you loved and cared for Abraham, Isaac and Jacob.' Then Moses spoke to the Israelites. 'Whoever wants to love God and follow his ways, come with me!'

112
God gives priests to help
Numbers 17—18

God listened to Moses and he gave the people another chance. The people who were willing to follow God's laws became God's special people. Then God gave them priests chosen from the descendants of Jacob's son, Levi. The priests were there to help them follow the Ten Commandments and to show them how to worship God. The priests also helped them to ask for God's forgiveness when they made mistakes or did bad things.

113
The ark of the covenant
Exodus 25:10—22

The agreement God made with Moses and the people was a covenant: God promised to take care of the people and they promised to keep his laws. God told Moses to put the special stones on which the Ten Commandments were written

into a wooden box trimmed with gold. It would be called the ark of the covenant. It had two gold rings on each side, so that it could be carried on poles wherever the Israelites went.

114
Twelve spies
Numbers 10—14

The Israelites walked through the desert for many years before they reached Canaan, the land God had promised them. Then Moses sent twelve spies into Canaan, one from each of the tribes descended from Jacob, to find out what kind of place it would be.

115
Living in the desert
Deuteronomy 31

Joshua and Caleb told everyone that God had given them a wonderful place to live. The land was full of sweet water and good things to eat. But the other ten spies said that the people in Canaan were fierce and frightening—and they were afraid! So the Israelites did not go to live in

Canaan. They stayed in the desert for many more years. Moses grew older and died before God's people made Canaan their home.

116
Joshua, the new leader
Joshua 1:1–9

Now the people needed a new leader. God chose Joshua, the man who had trusted God when the spies were first sent into Canaan. 'Don't worry about anything,' God told Joshua. 'I will always be there to help you just as I helped Moses. Be strong and brave. I will be with you wherever you go.'

117
More spies in Canaan
Joshua 2:1–7

There was a big city in Canaan called Jericho. It had strong high walls that kept the people inside safe and kept everyone else out. Anyone who wanted to live in Canaan had first to pass by Jericho. Joshua sent two spies into the city to find out about the people there. But the king found out. 'Quick! Hide here!' said Rahab. She hid the men under some flax which was drying on her roof while she sent the king's men another way. Rahab kept the spies safe until they could climb down the city wall and escape.

118
Rahab's new friends
Joshua 2:8–24

The spies were very grateful for Rahab's help. 'Everyone knows about the amazing things your God has done,' Rahab told them. 'We know God led you safely out of Egypt and we know God will

give you this land. I ask only this: be kind to my family. Save us as I have saved you.' The spies promised that her family would be kept safe, and gave her a red ribbon to mark her window.

119
Crossing the River Jordan
Joshua 3:1–17

The Israelites had to cross the River Jordan to reach Jericho, but there were no bridges or boats to get across and there were thousands of men, women and children. God told them what to do. The priests carrying the Ten Commandments walked into the river first. As soon as their feet touched the ground, God stopped the river flowing.

120
Safe on the other side
Joshua 3:17—4:18

The priests stood still on the river bed while all the men, women and children crossed over on dry land. God asked Joshua to choose a man from each tribe to carry a stone from the middle of the river. These twelve stones would always remind them of how God had helped them safely across the River Jordan. Then the priests crossed over too—and the waters of the River Jordan flowed back.

121
Help for Joshua
Joshua 5:13–15

Joshua went out alone to plan what they should do next. He saw the high walls of Jericho in front of him—it was a strong fortress. But he also saw a man with a sword in his hand. 'Who are you?' Joshua asked. 'I am the captain of God's army,' the man replied. Then Joshua knew that God would be there to help him as he had promised. Joshua fell to his knees as he realised that this man was an angel, God's messenger.

122
Loud-sounding trumpets!
Joshua 6:1–11

God spoke to Joshua through the angel and told him how they would take the city. It was a very strange plan... First the Israelites were to march around the city every day for six days while seven priests were to march in the middle of the army blowing trumpets made out of rams' horns.

123
Walls come tumbling down

Joshua 6:15–17

The people followed the battle plan and did everything God had told Joshua to do. On the seventh day, they marched around the city six times. On the seventh time, Joshua signalled for everyone to shout with all their might! And the walls of Jericho came tumbling down! The people of Jericho ran for their lives. But Rahab and her family knew that no one would hurt them. The spies kept their promise.

125
Deborah, the wise woman
Judges 4:4–10

For a while the people followed Joshua's advice and listened to God. But as time passed they forgot who God was. They forgot all the good things God had done for their ancestors. They forgot to ask him for help and forgot that God loved them. But God had not forgotten his people. He spoke to them through leaders called judges. Deborah was a wise woman, a prophetess and

124
The promised land
Joshua 23:14–16

God gave to Joshua and the Israelites the land of Canaan, where they could live safely. They spread out across the land to make their homes and they were happy. Joshua always listened to God and led his people well. Before he died, he encouraged them. 'God has kept all his promises to us. He loves his people. Keep his commandments always and he will bless you and take care of you.'

a judge. The Israelites would come to her and she would guide them to do the right thing. One day she told Barak that God wanted him to help his people by fighting the cruel Canaanite general, Sisera. But Barak was frightened. He didn't trust God to help him. 'I won't go unless you come with me,' he told Deborah.

126
Cowardly men
Judges 4:9–24

Deborah trusted God. 'I will come with you,' she told Barak, 'but because you will not trust God, it will not be you who wins this victory. It will be a woman who takes Sisera's life.' Deborah and Barak went into battle against Sisera and his 900 chariots. God made sure that the Israelites won the day. When his soldiers were losing the battle, Sisera escaped and hid in Jael's tent, a woman he thought was on his side. But Jael waited until he had fallen asleep, then she killed Sisera using a tent peg. When Barak came looking for Sisera, Jael showed him Sisera's dead body. Deborah had been right.

127
Men riding camels
Judges 6:11–35

For some time there was peace in the land because the Israelites learned to trust God again. But when they started to break God's rules, the Midianites attacked them, riding on camels. They stole their livestock and food and forced the Israelites to hide in caves. Years passed in this way until the people prayed to God to help them. Then God sent an angel to a man named Gideon. 'God has chosen you to lead the Israelites against the enemy!'

128
Gideon needs a sign
Judges 6:36–38

Gideon was hiding from the Midianites at the time. He thought the angel had made a mistake. Gideon looked around him. 'Me?' he said. 'Are you sure? I am not a soldier. I am not even a brave man. I am really no one at all!' The angel told him that it didn't matter. God would help Gideon if he would only trust him. Then Gideon asked for help. 'If you are sure, then will you help me believe? I will put a woolly fleece on the floor tonight. If there is dew on the fleece but not on the ground in the morning, I'll be sure you want me to do this.'

129
Gideon's fleece
Judges 6:39–40

When Gideon looked the next morning, his fleece was so wet, he could squeeze a whole bowl of water out of it! 'Please don't be angry with me,' Gideon said to God,

130
Gideon's huge army
Judges 7:2–5

Now Gideon was sure. He believed God wanted him to lead the army and he believed that God could make miracles happen. He gathered an army of over 30,000 men. 'Your army is too big!' God told Gideon. 'Send back anyone who is afraid.' A lot of people went home! Then Gideon took the men who were left down to the water. Some knelt down to drink while some scooped up the water in their hands.

'but this time, could you make the woolly fleece dry and the ground wet?' The next morning, the ground was wet with dew, but the fleece was perfectly dry.

132
God's victory

Judges 7:19–24

Gideon gave the signal and his men blew their horns and smashed the jars so that the light shone out. They shouted, 'A sword for the Lord and for Gideon!' The Midianites were so confused, they ran in fear for their lives! God had helped the Israelites to live safely in Canaan once more.

131
Gideon's small army

Judges 7:6–18

God told Gideon to choose for his army only the men who scooped up the water. The others were sent home. Now there were only 300 men left to fight against thousands... Gideon divided his men into three groups. He gave each man a trumpet and a jar with a torch inside. Then, in the middle of the night, they surrounded the Midianites.

133
Samson, the strong man

Judges 13:2–5, 24; 14:6

Again the people forgot the good things God had done. This time the Philistines came to make their lives difficult. God sent them a man called Samson, who wore his long hair in braids that had never been cut and was blessed with huge strength. Once he was attacked by a lion and

killed the beast with his bare hands. While Samson was blessed by God, the Philistines were afraid of him.

134
The final victory
Judges 16

Samson was in love with a woman called Delilah. The Philistines realised that she might be able to find out the secret of Samson's great strength, so they bribed Delilah with large sums of money. Delilah kept

asking Samson to tell her his secret until he could stand it no longer! If his hair was cut off, God would no longer bless him. Then Delilah betrayed Samson. While Samson slept, the Philistines cut off his hair, blinded him and took him away to prison. Samson could do nothing to stop them. His strength was gone. But God blessed Samson one last time. Samson waited until hundreds of Philistines had come together for a feast. Samson was tied to the pillars of the building. With one last effort, he pulled the pillars down and destroyed the people who had hurt the Israelites.

135
Ruth's kindness
Ruth 1:1–18

Naomi moved with her husband and sons to the land of Moab. After some time, her husband died; but Naomi still had her two sons to take care of her. Her sons married wives from Moab but then they also died, leaving the three women alone. Naomi was very sad and decided to go home to Bethlehem. 'Go back to your mothers,' she told her daughters-in-law. Orpah went home. But Ruth begged to stay with Naomi. 'Don't make me go,' she said. 'My home is with you now. I will go where you go and stay where you stay. Your people will be my people and I will worship your God.' Naomi was glad of Ruth's kindness. Naomi and Ruth went together to Bethlehem to make a new home there.

136
Ruth looks after Naomi
Ruth 2:1–3

Naomi was welcomed in her home town but Ruth had to go out into the fields to work so they would have enough to eat. God had made it part of the laws he gave to Moses that poor people could gather the leftover grain from the harvest so they would not be hungry. Ruth was happy to be busy and to look after her mother-in-law.

138
One happy family
Ruth 4:9–17

Boaz saw that Ruth was good and kind and loyal. They became friends, and Naomi knew that he wanted Ruth to be his wife. Naomi was very happy when Ruth and Boaz were married. She was even happier when later they made her a grandmother and she held her little grandson in her arms.

137
Boaz looks after Ruth
Ruth 2:4–12

Boaz was a relative of Naomi's and he owned the field where Ruth worked. When he heard how kind Ruth had been to stay with Naomi and take care of her, he spoke kindly to her. 'Gather as much grain as you need,' Boaz said. Then he told his men to leave more grain for her to pick up. When Naomi saw how much grain Ruth had collected, she knew that Boaz was a good man and that God had blessed them both.

139
Hannah's prayer

1 Samuel 1:1–20

Hannah wanted a baby very much. Everyone she knew had one baby and some had lots of babies—but although she and her husband loved each other very much, no babies came. Hannah prayed that God would bless them with a child; then she prayed that if she had a son she would let him train in the temple to serve God there all his life. She told Eli, the priest, that she was sad and had prayed to God. 'May God bless you, and give you what you have asked him,' Eli said.

140
God blesses Hannah

1 Samuel 1:21–28

God heard Hannah's prayers and blessed her with a baby son. She was the happiest wife in Israel when she gave birth to baby Samuel! Hannah loved him and looked after him well but when he was big enough, she took him to live in the temple just as she had promised. There Samuel learned how to love God and serve him with the help of Eli, the priest. Then God blessed Hannah with three sons and two daughters.

141
The call in the night
1 Samuel 3:1–9

One night, Samuel heard a voice calling him. He went to Eli and said, 'Here I am! You called me.' But Eli had been asleep. 'I didn't call you.

Go back to your bed.' A little while later, Samuel heard the voice again. Samuel went again to Eli—who sent him back to bed. When it happened a third time, Eli sat up and thought. 'God is speaking to you, Samuel,' he said. 'When he speaks to you again, answer him and tell him you are listening. God did call Samuel again. Samuel answered, and he listened. And God began to tell Samuel his plans for the people of Israel.

142
Samuel the prophet
1 Samuel 3:10–21

As the years passed, everyone knew they could trust Samuel because he listened when God spoke to him and he told them what God wanted them to do. They understood that what God wanted for them was good— he was like a father who takes good care of his children. With God's help, Samuel organised the Israelites into an army to stop the fierce Philistines from attacking them. For as long as Samuel was God's prophet there was peace in the land and the people were happy.

143
A king like everyone else
1 Samuel 3:4–22

When Samuel grew to be an old man, the people of Israel became worried about what would happen when he died. 'All the other nations around us have a king,' they said. 'Choose a king to rule us when you are gone.' Samuel was unhappy about this. He asked God what to do. 'Tell them what will happen when they have a king. If they still want one, we will listen.' So Samuel told the people that a king would take their sons away into battle or to work his fields; he would take their best land and some of what they grew in taxes. 'God is your king!' Samuel told them. 'Trust him.'

144
The lost donkeys
1 Samuel 9:1–10

The people would not listen to Samuel. 'We want a king!' they said. So God told Samuel to choose a king for them. Samuel waited for God to tell him the man to choose. Then one day, a man named Saul came to him. 'Can you tell me where to find Samuel, the prophet?' Saul asked him. Saul had come out to find his father's donkeys. They had wandered off somewhere and Saul had been searching for days so that he could bring them home. Samuel smiled.

145
Samuel anoints Saul

1 Samuel 9:22—10:1

When Samuel saw the tall, handsome man coming towards him, God told him that Saul would be the people's king. 'I am Samuel,' he told Saul. 'I have been waiting for you. Come with me—we have a feast prepared! God has some special plans for you. And don't worry about your father's donkeys—they have been found.' Saul was amazed. 'But why? I am no one—I am less than no one!' But he sat down to a feast with Samuel that day. Before Saul left for the journey home, Samuel took Saul to one side and poured holy oil on his head. 'Now you are the anointed king of Israel. It will be your job to lead God's people and look after them.'

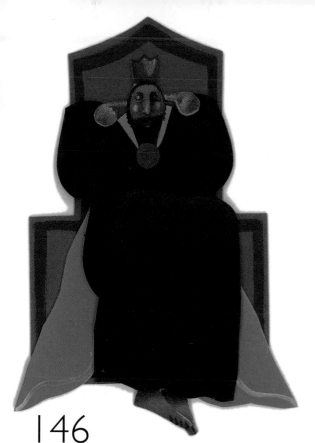

146
The people's king
1 Samuel 10:17–27

A week later, Samuel gathered the twelve tribes to show them their new king. 'You asked for a king to help you; you decided God was not enough. Now—here he is.' But Saul could not be found. He was so worried, he was hiding! But when Saul stood up in front of everyone, they were delighted with the king God had chosen. 'Long live the king!' they shouted.

147
Saul knows best
1 Samuel 15:1–35

God blessed Saul to help him be a good king. At first everyone was happy. Saul listened to God and led his people well. Soon they were respected among the nations around them and people were afraid to fight them. King Saul was popular. Samuel was pleased. 'I will pray for you,' he told the people. 'Don't forget how God has taken care of you in the past and remember to love him and follow the Ten Commandments. Then God will bless you.' But after some time, Saul forgot that he was God's king. He knew the people loved him. He began to think that he didn't need to do things God's way at all. He began to think he didn't need God's help. Then he stopped listening to God. He did as he liked. Samuel was disappointed. 'What have you done?' he asked Saul. 'If you will not listen to God, he will find another man who will...'

148
A new king for Israel

1 Samuel 16:1–9

Samuel knew that God wanted a good king, a man who would be wise and do what was right—not just a powerful man. So he wasn't surprised when God sent him to Bethlehem to meet a man named Jesse, who had eight sons. Jesse introduced the eldest of his sons. He was tall and strong and handsome. 'This must be the one God has chosen,' Samuel thought. But God told Samuel that this was not the right man to be king of Israel.

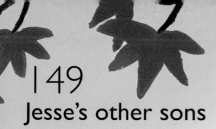

149
Jesse's other sons
1 Samuel 16:9–11

Jesse introduced his second son. He was also tall and strong and handsome. But God told Samuel that he was not his chosen king. Samuel met Jesse's third, fourth, fifth, sixth and seventh sons. They were all tall and strong and handsome but none of them was God's chosen king. 'What a person looks like on the outside is not everything,' said God. 'What matters is whether they are good and kind and wise. I see what people are like when no one is looking at them.' So Samuel asked Jesse, 'Do you have another son?'

150
God chooses David
1 Samuel 16:12–13

Jesse was surprised that none of his sons had been the man that Samuel was looking for. But he did have one more son. 'My youngest son, David, is taking care of the sheep. I will send someone for him.' When Samuel met David, God said, 'This is the next king of Israel.' So Samuel anointed David with oil, as a sign that one day he would be king.

151
Sleepless nights
1 Samuel 16:14–18

King Saul couldn't sleep. He was grumpy and cross. He shouted at everyone. No one could do anything right. Then one of his servants said, 'Perhaps some music would help you sleep. I know a young man who loves God and plays music on the harp. His name is David.'

152
Saul meets David
Psalm 23

So David came to Saul's court to play his harp for the king. Saul liked David and his music soothed the king so much that he decided to give him a job. 'David can take care of my armour,' he said. 'Then he can be here whenever I need him.' David wrote words to go with his music. 'God is my shepherd,' he sang. 'He gives me everything I need. Nothing can frighten me, because God will always take care of me.'

153
A giant called Goliath
1 Samuel 17:1–11

The Philistine army was always bothering the Israelites. They had a champion, a huge man named Goliath. Day by day, Goliath marched up and down and shouted at them. 'Is no one brave enough to stand against me?' he boomed. 'Come out and fight me!' David heard the giant's challenge; and he saw that his brothers, who were soldiers, and even the king himself, trembled when they heard Goliath.

154
David fights the giant
1 Samuel 17:31–58

'Why are you afraid?' David asked them. 'If no one else will go, I will fight this bully!' King Saul offered David his armour but it was too big and heavy for him. He took his sling

and found some stones from the stream. 'He may have fancy armour, but I have the God of all the world to help me!' he said. Then David swung the sling around his head. The stone hit Goliath in the forehead and the giant fell down with a thud. The Israelites cheered. David had defeated Goliath!

155
The people's hero
1 Samuel 18:6–9; 2 Samuel 5:1–5

At first Saul was pleased that David had beaten the Philistine champion. But when everyone started telling stories about David's bravery and singing songs about him, Saul became very jealous. Saul's son, Jonathan, was David's best friend. Even Jonathan warned David to stay away from the king. Then Saul found that the people were divided. Some were on Saul's side and others on David's. Saul tried to kill David several times but David would not hurt the man God had chosen as king. The man who had once been David's friend was now his enemy.

156
The king in Jerusalem
2 Samuel 6:1–19

When Saul died, the people asked David to be their king. They loved him. He was not only strong and brave but he was a king of Israel who loved God and did good things. For a while, there was peace again in the land. David took the ark of the

covenant to the city of Jerusalem and made this the place where he lived.

157
A very big mistake
2 Samuel 11:1–27

One night, while David's army was away at war, David saw a beautiful woman from his rooftop. He found out that she was Bathsheba, the wife of Uriah, one of his soldiers. David wanted very much to meet Bathsheba. Then, when he had met her, he decided he couldn't live without her. He wanted her to be his wife. David sent a message to one of his commanders to make sure that Uriah was in the most dangerous part of the battlefield so that he would be killed. Then, when the news came that Uriah was dead, he married Bathsheba. It was a terrible thing to do. It was David's first big mistake.

158
Nathan tells a story
2 Samuel 12:1–7

David knew that he had stolen another man's wife and arranged his death. He knew he had done something very wrong and hoped no one else would find out. But God knew what David had done. God sent Nathan the prophet to David. Nathan told David a story about a very rich man who had everything—but still stole a poor man's only lamb. David was angry. 'That rich man deserves to die!' David said. Nathan looked David in the eye. 'But you are that rich man,' he said.

159
David is sorry
2 Samuel 12:13

Then David saw for the first time that he had done something terrible. He had stolen Bathsheba from her husband and arranged his death just because she was beautiful and he was the king. David had abused his power and behaved very badly—just as if he didn't know or love God at all. David put his head in his hands and he cried. David told God that he was very, very sorry.

160
God forgives
2 Samuel 12:13–24

'God is very sad because of what you have done,' said Nathan. 'But God will not hold this against you for ever. God will forgive you.' Not long afterwards, Bathsheba gave birth to a baby son who became ill and died. Then God blessed David and Bathsheba with another son and David began to be happy again. They named their son Solomon.

161
A rival king
2 Samuel 13—18

David had married other wives before Bathsheba. He also had other sons. Absalom wanted to be king very much—so much that he and his soldiers went to war with David. Absalom was riding through the forest when his long hair got stuck in a tree. One of David's soldiers found him there and killed him. David loved Absalom very much even though he had caused so much trouble. He was very sad when he heard that his son was dead.

162
The next king of Israel

2 Samuel 22:1; 1 Kings 1:31–37

David wrote many poems and songs during the time when he was king. Some were happy and told God how great he was. In others David asked for God's help. Before he died he

asked to see Bathsheba and Nathan. 'I want you to make sure Solomon is the next king,' he said.

163
David's advice

1 Kings 1:38–40; 2:1–12

Solomon came to see his father. David wanted Solomon to be a great king—a king even better than he had been himself. 'God promised me that my son would be king after me,' David told him. 'Now it is time for me to die. Be brave and strong and remember to keep God's commandments, Solomon. Listen to God and do as he says and you will succeed in everything you do.' Then Solomon was anointed with oil and declared king.

164
A gift for Solomon
1 Kings 3:5–15

Solomon wanted to do what was right and he tried to follow God's laws. But he was young. One night in a dream, God said to Solomon, 'Ask for anything you like and I will give it to you.' Some men would have asked to be rich or famous or to live a long and happy life. But Solomon prayed: 'Please give me a wise heart, so I can help your people and lead them well.' God was so pleased with Solomon's answer that he made him wise, rich and famous! Soon people everywhere had heard about his wisdom.

165
Solomon, the wise king
1 Kings 3:16–28

One day two women came to see Solomon. Both women had given birth to baby boys. One baby had died. 'The living baby is mine!' said one. 'No, he's mine!' said the other. Solomon knew how he could find out who the real mother was. 'Cut the baby in half,' Solomon said. 'Then you can share it.' One of the women said, 'Yes, cut the baby in half!' The other said, 'No! She can have the baby—but let him live!' Solomon gave the baby to the second woman. Then everyone knew that God had made Solomon a wise king.

166
A beautiful temple
1 Kings 5:13—6:38

David had always wanted to build a house for God to show how much he loved him. But it was Solomon who built the temple. It

took thousands of men seven years to build it. Solomon made it with stone walls panelled with wood and covered in gold. It was decorated with carved flowers and golden angels. It was beautiful.

167
Solomon's prayer
1 Kings 8:22–66

Solomon prayed in front of all the people. 'Lord, you are great and wonderful and kind. I know you are too great to live in this temple. But let your people come to worship you here. Let this be the place where they can come to ask for your help in their need, and for your forgiveness when they do things that are wrong.'

168
The queen of Sheba
1 Kings 10:1–13

A queen from the faraway land of Sheba came to find out whether all the things she had heard about Solomon were true. When she saw his palace and heard the wise things he said, she gave Solomon gifts of gold, precious stones and spices. 'God really has blessed you,' she told him.

169
Ahab and Jezebel
1 Kings 16:29–33

After Solomon died, there were kings of Israel who did not love God. King Ahab married a woman named Jezebel who worshipped a false god called Baal. Ahab built a temple to Baal and worshipped the false god too. Ahab broke many of God's ten commandments.

170
Elijah and the drought
1 Kings 17:1

God wanted to give Ahab a chance to change so he sent his prophet, Elijah, with a message. 'God is the only true and living God. But you worship gods of wood and stone who can do nothing. Now God has decided that unless you change your ways and keep his commandments, he will send no more rain.'

171
Ravens bring food
1 Kings 17:2–6

King Ahab was very angry. Elijah was so afraid the king would kill him that he ran away! God told him where

he could get water from a brook to drink. Then God sent ravens to Elijah with bread each morning and with bread and meat each evening. God took care of Elijah.

172
The widow
1 Kings 17:7–12

When the brook dried up in the drought, God told Elijah to go to a village where a widow would help him. Elijah met the widow gathering sticks to make a fire and asked for food. 'I am about to make bread for the last meal we will eat before we die,' she said.

173
God provides
1 Kings 17:13–16

'Share your food with me now and trust God,' Elijah told the widow. So she did. She used the last of her flour and her last drop of oil to make bread for Elijah. But when she looked again, there was enough flour and oil for more bread! God provided for Elijah and the widow's family until rain fell once more upon the earth.

174
Will you love God?
1 Kings 18:16–18

Three years had passed. Still it had not rained and the earth was dry and cracked. Elijah went to see King Ahab. 'Well? Have you had enough?' Elijah

asked the king. 'Are you ready yet to tell God you are sorry? Will you stop worshipping Baal and love God instead?'

175
Time to choose
1 Kings 18:19–23

Elijah told King Ahab to gather all the prophets of Baal and meet on top of Mount Carmel. Then Elijah spoke to the Israelites gathered there. 'It is time to choose. Who will you worship? Who is the true and living God? If the Lord is God, then follow

176
No answer from Baal
I Kings 18:22–29

'Ask your god to light your altar with fire,' Elijah said. 'If he does, he must be the true god.' The prophets of Baal danced and shouted, shouted and danced, but nothing happened; nothing at all. 'Perhaps your god is on holiday? Or is he asleep? Shout louder.' But nothing came from Baal. No fire lit the altar.

him. But if Baal is god, then follow him.' Elijah challenged the prophets of Baal to prepare a sacrifice to their god while Elijah did the same.

177
Elijah's altar
1 Kings 18:30–35

Then Elijah built an altar of twelve stones, one for each tribe of Israel. He made a small trench around the altar. 'Fill four jars of water and pour them over the wood of this altar. Do it again and again until everything is soaking wet.' The water flowed over Elijah's altar and filled the trench. Surely no fire could burn up Elijah's sacrifice now?

178
God answers Elijah
1 Kings 18:36–45

'Show these people that you alone are God,' Elijah prayed. 'Answer me and light up this altar with fire.' Suddenly fire fell from heaven and burned the wet wood on the altar. God had answered Elijah and shown all the people that he was the true and living God. The people knelt down and worshipped him. Then they saw a little cloud appear in the sky, then bigger rain clouds. The drought was over.

179
Elijah's helper
1 Kings 19:14–21

Elijah was sometimes lonely. He asked God for someone to help him. God sent him to find Elisha, who was ploughing in the fields near his home. Elisha was happy to leave his home to help Elijah serve God. Soon people knew that Elisha would be God's prophet when Elijah died. God would speak through him.

180
Chariot of fire
2 Kings 2:1–11

Elisha worked with Elijah for some time. He knew Elijah was now an old man. 'Stay here,' Elijah told Elisha one day. But Elisha would not leave him. They were at the River Jordan, and Elijah divided the water for them to cross on dry land. Suddenly, a chariot of fire drawn by horses carried Elijah away to heaven in a whirlwind. Elijah had gone and God blessed Elisha with his power.

Naaman had a skin disease called leprosy. It gave him white patches all over his skin. 'I wish my master would visit the prophet Elisha in the land of my home,' she whispered to her mistress. 'I am sure that God could cure my master.'

182
A letter for the king
2 Kings 5:1–10

Naaman's wife told him there might be hope for him. So Naaman took a letter to the king of Israel asking him to cure his leprosy. The king was very frightened. 'How can I do that?' shouted the king. 'Am I God?! This is an excuse to make war upon me!' But Elisha heard what had happened, and told the king to send Naaman to him. 'I will show him that the living God lives in Israel!'

181
The little servant girl
2 Kings 5:1–3

An Israelite girl had been taken captive to work as a servant in the house of Naaman, a captain of the Aramean army. The girl noticed that

183
Washing in the River Jordan

2 Kings 5:9–14

Naaman went to see Elisha. He stopped outside his door with his horses and chariots. But Elisha did not go out to see him. Instead he sent his servant with a message for Naaman. 'Go and wash seven times in the River Jordan and you will be healed.' Naaman had expected Elisha to come and pray for him or wave his hands over Naaman's skin. He was not happy to have been treated as if he was not important. And why wash in the dirty River Jordan? There were better rivers where he came from! But Naaman's servant encouraged him. 'If the prophet had asked you to do something difficult you would have done it,' he reasoned. 'Why not see if this will heal you?' So Naaman washed seven times—and his skin was whole and new again. God had healed him.

184
God speaks to Jonah
Jonah 1:1–2

A long time after Elisha had died, God spoke through a prophet called Jonah. 'I have seen the terrible things that the people of Nineveh do,' God said. 'Go to Nineveh and warn the people there that they must change their ways—or terrible things will happen to them,' said God. The people of Nineveh were cruel and keen on fighting. Jonah did not want to go! But Jonah also felt they were bad people who deserved any punishment that came to them. He knew that God was loving and forgiving.

185
The prophet runs away
Jonah 1:3

Jonah went down to the port at Joppa and boarded a ship heading for Tarshish—about as far in the opposite direction as he could go. He paid his fare and then found somewhere below deck to hide away—and Jonah fell asleep. But Jonah had forgotten that you can't hide from God.

186
A terrible storm
Jonah 1:4–6

A great wind blew and tore at the ship's sails. Huge rolling waves rocked the ship up and down dangerously and water sloshed over the sides. The ship sailing for

Tarshish suddenly found itself in the middle of a violent storm. The sailors were so afraid, they threw the cargo overboard to save themselves. They woke the sleeping Jonah and demanded that he pray for help. 'Is this anything to do with you?' they asked him. 'Who are you and where do you come from?' Then Jonah knew what had happened. 'I am a Hebrew and I worship the living God who made the land and sea. But I have run away because I didn't want to obey him. This storm is all my fault.'

187
The sailors decide…
Jonah 1:9–12

The waves were whooshing higher and higher and the wind was howling. The sailors were now terrified. 'What shall we do?' they shouted, clinging on for their lives. Jonah knew the answer. 'Pick me up and throw me over the side,' he shouted back, 'then the sea will be calm again.' The sailors tried to row back to land because they didn't want to hurt Jonah—but the sea grew wilder. So the sailors threw Jonah overboard…

188
Down in the deep blue sea
Jonah 1:15–17

Jonah fell down, down, down into the deep blue sea and God stilled the raging storm. The sailors realised how great Jonah's God was because he could cause and calm a storm, and they fell to their knees in awe of him. Then God sent a great big sea creature to swallow Jonah whole. The prophet sat in the belly of the creature for three days and three nights. Jonah knew that God had saved him.

189
Jonah prays to God
Jonah 2:1–10

Jonah prayed to God from inside the body of the sea creature. 'I needed help and you were there for me, Lord! I thought I was dying but you rescued me. When I was surrounded by water and seaweed was wrapped around my head, you saved me. Thank you for giving me another chance. I am your prophet: I promised to serve you and I will, because only you have the power to save!' Then God told the creature to spit Jonah out on to dry land.

190
A message from God
Jonah 3:1–5

This time when God told Jonah to go to Nineveh with his warning for the people, Jonah went. As he approached the great city, he shouted out, 'God says that in 40 days Nineveh will be destroyed!' It took three days for Jonah to reach all the people with the message, from the shopkeepers and soldiers to the king in his palace. The cruel people of Nineveh did not attack Jonah; they did not ignore him or laugh at him. Instead they stopped and listened and acted on God's message. They stopped feasting and partying; they stopped bullying and fighting; and they started to pray.

191
The people are sorry
Jonah 3:5–10

The people of Nineveh told God they were sorry for all the cruel things they had said and done; for all the acts of violence against other nations. They did not know if it were possible to change God's mind but they hoped he would be kind and forgive them. Everyone in Nineveh stopped eating and drinking to show God they really were sorry. Even the king of Nineveh tore off his beautiful robes and wore itchy sackcloth to show God how sorry he was. God heard the prayers of the people of Nineveh and he saw that they were trying to change their ways. God saw that they really were sorry. The terrible things that Jonah had warned would happen did not happen because God, who is kind and loving and caring and forgiving, forgave them.

192
God's kindness

Jonah 4:1–11

Jonah went to a quiet place in the shade of a vine to sit and watch the people of Nineveh. Jonah was not happy: he thought they deserved to die. When the vine withered and died, Jonah was even more unhappy. 'Jonah,' said God, 'you didn't grow or take care of that vine, but you cared when it died. I did make these people and I care what happens to them. Can you understand that?'

193
Jeremiah, a young prophet
Jeremiah 1:1–10

Jeremiah was still very young when God chose him to be his prophet many years after Jonah. The people had again forgotten his commandments. They worshipped false gods—again! 'I loved you even before you were born,' said God. 'I saw you when you were growing in your mother's womb. I have plans for you and I will help you. Go to the people and speak for me. I will tell you what to say. Trust me, Jeremiah.'

194
At the potter's house

Jeremiah 18:1–6

God sent Jeremiah to a potter's house. Jeremiah watched as the potter's wheel spun around and around. First the clay made a round useful pot but then it wobbled a little and became a strange shape, good for nothing. The potter took the clay and reshaped it to make a beautiful pot. Jeremiah saw that God was like the potter and his people were like the clay. Even if things had gone wrong, God could change his people into something better.

195
The king won't listen

Jeremiah 36:1–28

Jeremiah started to tell God's people that they should listen to God and keep his commandments; they should love him and worship him again. But no one listened. Then Jeremiah asked his friend Baruch to write down everything God told him on a long scroll. This time the king's officials listened. They told King Jehoiakim that he must hear the words too. But as each part of the scroll was read out to him, the king sliced off that part of the scroll and threw it into the fire. When the whole scroll was burned, he sent people to arrest Jeremiah and Baruch. But they knew they were in danger—and they had hidden themselves away! Then Jeremiah sat down with Baruch… and began writing down God's words all over again.

197
A deep, dark prison

Jeremiah 37:11–21

Jeremiah had bought a piece of land outside the city walls. For a little while it was quiet outside the city because the Babylonians had withdrawn. So Jeremiah planned to go and look at the land. But when the captain of the guard saw him, he arrested him. 'Where do you think you are going?' he demanded. 'You are deserting us and going over to the Babylonians!' Nothing Jeremiah said would change his mind. So Jeremiah was beaten and put into a dark cell in a dungeon. He was there a long time and was

196
God's warning

Jeremiah 37:6–10

God spoke to Jeremiah again. 'I know that the king is waiting to hear from me—so go to him and warn him. Tell him the Egyptians will not help him. Instead the Babylonians will come and attack the city. They will not rest until they have captured the people and burned the city to the ground.'

very unhappy. Then one day the king sent for him. Jeremiah was brought to the palace where the king asked him secretly if God had given him another message. 'Yes, he has. Soon the Babylonians will come and capture you,' said Jeremiah. 'But please—don't send me back to prison or I will die!'

198
Stuck in the mud
Jeremiah 37:21—38:6

The king had Jeremiah moved to the palace courtyard but Jeremiah could not keep quiet. He told anyone who would listen that they should surrender to the Babylonians—or they would die. When the king's officials heard him, they were very angry. 'This man is upsetting everyone!' they said. Then they threw Jeremiah into an empty well and left him there to die. Jeremiah sank deep into the mud at the bottom.

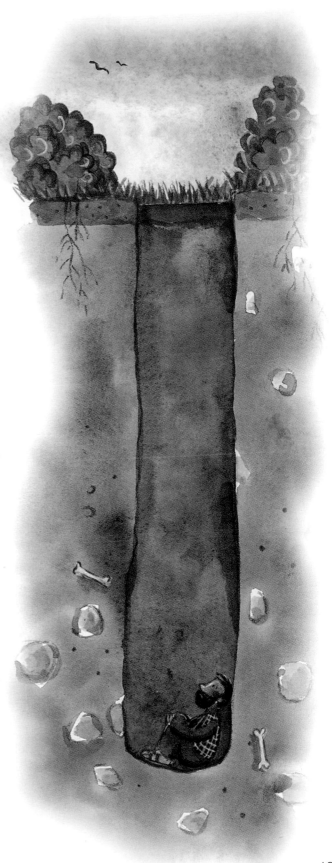

199
Hope for Jeremiah
Jeremiah 38:7–13

Ebed-Melech heard what had happened to Jeremiah and saw how miserable he was. He went to see the king. 'My Lord the king, your men have done terrible things to Jeremiah. He will starve to death if you leave him in that well! Please do something to save him—he doesn't deserve this.' So the king let Ebed-Melech take 30 men to pull Jeremiah out of the well. He found some old clothes and told Jeremiah to put them under his arms so the ropes would not cut and burn him. Then they pulled him to safety.

200
The fall of Jerusalem
Jeremiah 38:17—39:7

When the king saw Jeremiah again he demanded good news—but the prophet had none to give. 'I can only tell you what God tells me, and you won't listen!' he said. 'God says you must surrender to the Babylonians—it is too late to do anything else. Do this and you will live.' But the king wouldn't trust God. When the Babylonians captured Jerusalem, they killed the king's sons and blinded him before taking him away in chains.

201
Slavery and freedom

Jeremiah 39:8—40:6

Now the walls of Jerusalem had been broken down and the palace had burned to the ground; Solomon's beautiful temple was in ruins and the precious things inside had been stolen. Many of the people had been taken in chains to Babylon to work for the king there. But the Babylonian commander came looking for Jeremiah. 'Your God said all this would happen,' he said, 'because your people would not listen to him. But you have done nothing wrong, Jeremiah. You are free. You can come with me or you can stay.' Jeremiah chose to stay behind with the poor people who needed his help.

of all the young men, they were trained for three years to work in the palace of the king. At first they were offered meat and wine from the king's table to eat. Daniel knew that it had been offered first to the pretend gods the Babylonians worshipped and he did not want to break God's commandments. He asked if they could have vegetables and water instead.

202
Living in Babylon
Daniel 1:1–16

Daniel, Shadrach, Meshach and Abednego were among the people taken to Babylon from Jerusalem. As they were the brightest and best

203
The king's bad dream
Daniel 2:1–12

God blessed the four young men with knowledge and understanding. He also gave Daniel the power to understand the meaning of dreams. Now King Nebuchadnezzar started

He asked for more time so that he would be able to help him. Then he went to his three friends. 'We must pray!' said Daniel. 'Plead with God so that we will know the mystery of what the king dreamed and then what that dream means.' That night God answered their prayers. Then Daniel praised God. 'You know everything, Lord, and you are good and kind to tell us now what no man could ever know. Thank you!' Then Daniel went to see King Nebuchadnezzar.

to have bad dreams that kept him awake at night. His magicians said, 'Tell us your dreams and we will tell you what they mean.' But the king said, 'No! If you're so clever, tell me what I dreamed first—or you will all die!' The magicians trembled. They knew they couldn't. 'But there is no man alive who can do this!' they said. 'Only God knows what dreams men have.' The king was very angry. 'Then prepare to die!' he said.

204
Only God knows
Daniel 2:13–23

When the men came to arrest Daniel and his friends, Daniel asked if he could see the king.

and he has answered me. Now I can show you his power by telling you what you dreamed. You saw a strong statue that was hit by a rock and smashed into a million pieces. Then the rock became a great mountain. God is warning you that although you are now a great king who is in control of a great nation, one day, others will come and destroy you and you will have no power. Finally, God's kingdom, which will never end, will come and all the nations on earth will know that God alone is king.' Then the king thanked Daniel. 'Your God really is great—and can reveal hidden mysteries,' he said.

205
The end of the mystery
Daniel 2:26–47

'Can you tell me what I dreamed?' the king asked. 'No wise man or magician on earth can tell you your dream,' Daniel replied, 'but there is a God in heaven who can. I have prayed to him for help

206
The king's short memory
Daniel 2:48—3:22

King Nebuchadnezzar gave Daniel and his friends important jobs in his kingdom because he was so pleased with Daniel. But he soon forgot God's warning. He made a huge golden statue of himself. 'Everyone in the kingdom must bow down and worship my statue!' he said. But Shadrach, Meshach and Abednego would worship only God. So they were thrown into a fiery furnace.

207
The power to save
Daniel 3:24—29

'Who is that in the fire?' said the king. 'Surely only three men were thrown in?' The king had seen a fourth man, an angel, sent by God to protect Shadrach, Meshach and Abednego. King Nebuchadnezzar ordered the three men to come out of the fire. They were completely unhurt—they didn't even smell smoky! Then he praised God, who had the power to save them.

that his father had stolen from the temple in Jerusalem. He didn't care where they had come from. He didn't care that they had once been used in the temple of the living God.

208
A new king in Babylon
Daniel 5:1–2

When King Nebuchadnezzar died, his son Belshazzar became king. Daniel was now an old man and no one wanted him at court. Belshazzar did not even know Daniel. Then one day the king threw a party for a thousand of the most important people in Babylon. He decided to use the beautiful gold and silver goblets

209
The writing on the wall
Daniel 5:3–7

While King Belshazzar and his guests drank wine from the beautiful goblets, and praised the gods they believed in, of gold and silver, wood and stone, the king's face suddenly went pale with fear. He stared at the wall in front of him where words appeared, written by the hand of an invisible man. Everyone turned to look at the strange words. They could hardly believe their eyes! The event had turned from a celebration into a horrible nightmare.

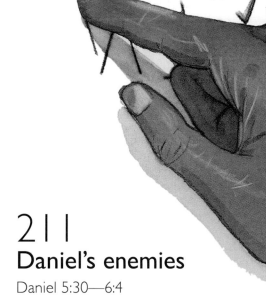

210
Where is Daniel?
Daniel 5:13–29

The king did not know the meaning of the words. None of the people in the room could understand them either. 'Bring me all the wise men of the kingdom!' the king shouted. 'Let someone explain to me what these words mean and I will reward them richly.' None of the king's magicians knew what the message said. No one could help. Then the king became even more frightened until the queen came into the room. 'Don't be afraid,' she said. 'When your father was king he trusted a man who understood the mind of God. He will help you. His name is Daniel.' So they found Daniel and he came to explain the meaning of the words on the wall. 'God has counted the days you will be king,' Daniel read. 'They are over! God has tested you, and you have not passed the test. Now your kingdom will be given to the Medes and the Persians.'

211
Daniel's enemies
Daniel 5:30—6:4

All that Daniel said came true. That very night, Belshazzar was killed and Darius the Mede became king. Then King Darius appointed Daniel as one of many men who would help to rule his kingdom. He was so pleased with everything Daniel did that he gave him even more power... So Daniel had a great friend—but he also made plenty of enemies, men who were jealous of the power he had been given. The men began to plot to find a way to get Daniel into trouble but Daniel was such a good man that they could find nothing.

212
Plots against Daniel
Daniel 6:5–9

How could they make Daniel do something wrong? They knew that Daniel loved God so they began to form a clever plan. They told King Darius how great he was. They persuaded the king to pass a law. If someone prayed to anyone but him, that person would be thrown into a den of lions!

213
Daniel prays
Daniel 6:10–15

What would Daniel do? Daniel did what he did every day. He went home and prayed to God. His enemies' plot had worked! Daniel had broken the new law. They could not wait to tell the king. Then Darius was very sad. He did not want to hurt Daniel, but he knew that he had made the law and the law could not be changed.

214
Daniel in the lions' den
Daniel 6:16–20

Daniel was marched away and thrown into a den of lions. The door was locked tight. 'Grrrr!' went the hungry beasts. King Darius shouted through the door, 'May your God save you, Daniel!' The king was so worried that he could not eat that evening and he could not sleep that night. In the morning he hurried to the lions' den. 'Has your God been able to save you from the lions, Daniel?' he called through the door.

215
God saves Daniel
Daniel 6:21–28

Then a voice came from inside the lions' den. 'God sent his angel to shut the lions' mouths,' said Daniel. 'The lions have not hurt me at all.' King Darius made sure Daniel was released from the den. Then he issued a new law. 'From now on, all people should respect Daniel's God, because he alone has the power to save, even from the mouths of lions.'

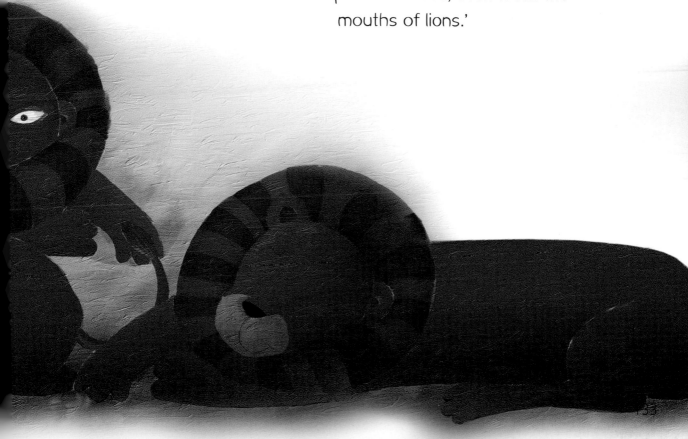

216
Nehemiah's prayer
Nehemiah 1:2–11

Nehemiah was cupbearer to King Artaxerxes in Babylon. It was many years since the Israelites had lived in Jerusalem together but one day his brother came with news about the people who still lived there. It made Nehemiah very sad to hear that the place he once called home was in ruins. He wept when he heard the news. Then Nehemiah prayed to God. 'Lord, you are great and awesome—there is no one else like you. I know you love your people, even though they have failed to obey you and disappointed you. Now please help me as I talk to the king. Make it possible for me to return to Jerusalem and make it home once more.'

217
The king helps Nehemiah
Nehemiah 2:1–8

The king saw how sad his cupbearer looked. 'What's wrong, Nehemiah?'

he asked. Then Nehemiah told him the news and said he wanted to go home to Jerusalem and rebuild its walls and gates. The king not only said Nehemiah could go, he sent him with special letters so he could buy supplies to do the work!

218
Broken walls are mended
Nehemiah 2:9—6:19

Nehemiah went to Jerusalem and planned what could be done. He encouraged the people there, telling them all how God had answered his prayers. The people suddenly realised that things could change. They believed that God would help them. They worked with Nehemiah to repair the walls of Jerusalem and built new city gates. When they were afraid their enemies would attack them, Nehemiah reminded them that God was on their side. Together they fixed the walls in only 52 days!

219
The Israelites weep
Nehemiah 8:1–12

As the people of Jerusalem came together inside the walls, Ezra the priest read to them the laws God had given to Moses. He reminded the people of God's love for them. They wept when they realised how they had disappointed God. Then they thanked him for bringing them home.

220
A ruler from Bethlehem
Micah 5:2–5

It had been a long journey from the first time people disobeyed God in the garden of Eden until now. God sent the prophet Micah to tell his people that he would send someone to be like a shepherd to them, who

would love them and take care of them. When he was born in the little town of Bethlehem, he would bring them peace. God would send someone to save them. They just had to wait till that time came.

221
Elizabeth and Zechariah
Luke 1:5–7

In the time when Herod was king of Judea, God's prophecies about a saviour for his people began to come true. God made Zechariah, the priest, and his wife, Elizabeth, part of his plan. Elizabeth and Zechariah were good people and they loved God. But they had one great sadness—they were now quite old but had no children. They had both asked God to bless them with a baby to love but nothing had happened. Now all that was about to change.

222
A visit from an angel
Luke 1:8–22

It was Zechariah's turn to burn incense in the temple while everyone was outside praying. Suddenly Zechariah saw an angel appear beside the altar. He was very frightened! 'Don't be afraid, Zechariah,' said the angel. 'I am here to tell you that God has heard your prayers and soon you will be blessed with a baby son. Call him John. He will be no ordinary child because God has chosen him to prepare the people for his chosen saviour.' Zechariah could hardly believe the message of the angel. 'Are you sure?' he asked. 'Both my wife and I are old now— probably too old to have children of our own.' The angel replied, 'I am the angel Gabriel and God has sent me with this message. All this will happen as I have said but until then you will lose your voice because you didn't trust me.' The people outside the temple were worried. Where was Zechariah? But when he came out, unable to speak, they realised he had seen a vision. A little while later, Elizabeth told him that she was expecting a baby…

223
Gabriel visits Mary
Luke 1:26–38

Elizabeth had a young cousin called Mary who was going to marry Joseph, a carpenter. Mary lived in Nazareth in the area around Lake Galilee. Six months after Gabriel had been to see Zechariah, he went to visit Mary. She was frightened to see an angel in her home. 'Don't be afraid,' said Gabriel. 'God has chosen to bless you, Mary. You will have a child named Jesus, and he will be called the son of God himself.' Mary was very surprised at this news. 'But I'm not married yet,' she said. 'Don't worry, Mary. Nothing is impossible for God. Trust him. Elizabeth is also expecting a baby and everyone said that was impossible too.' Mary thought for a moment. 'I love God,' she said. 'I am ready to do whatever he wants of me.' Then the angel Gabriel left Mary.

224
Mary visits Elizabeth
Luke 1:39–45

Mary had to tell someone about the angel's message. She thought Elizabeth would understand. Mary travelled into the hills where Elizabeth lived. 'Hello!' Mary called as she drew near. When Elizabeth heard Mary's voice, the baby inside her kicked with joy! 'I'm so lucky that the mother of the Saviour is here visiting me!' said Elizabeth. 'God has done something very wonderful and you are amazing, Mary, because you are willing to trust God by having this special baby.' Mary was so happy that she praised God, telling him how wonderful he was—to choose a young country girl to be the mother of his son.

225
Elizabeth's little boy
Luke 1:57–66

Mary stayed with Elizabeth for three happy months. After she had gone home, Elizabeth gave birth to her own little son. Just as Gabriel had told them, they named him John. Zechariah, who had been quiet for so long, then found he could speak once more. Zechariah knew now that God had special plans for John. He was also part of God's plan. He would tell people that the saviour was coming! He would tell them to get ready for something amazing to happen.

to him. 'Don't worry, Joseph. Marry Mary just as you had planned. She needs you to help take care of God's son.' When Joseph woke up, he was not so sad any more. God had given him an important job to do.

226
Joseph is sad
Matthew 1:18–25

Joseph loved Mary. He had planned to marry her; but now she was telling him stories about an angel… and she was pregnant. Joseph knew it was not his baby but Mary had said she was carrying God's son. Could her story be true? He was worried people would say unkind things about her. Then one night Joseph dreamed that an angel spoke

227
The Roman census
Luke 2:1–5

In those days, the Israelites were ruled by the Roman emperor. Soldiers marched about their towns and villages. Now Caesar Augustus had issued an order that everyone should return to the place where their families came from to be counted. Then he could tax all his people. So Joseph took Mary with him to Bethlehem, the city where King David had lived long, long ago.

228
No room at the inn
Luke 2:6–7

Lots of people had come to Bethlehem for the census. The streets were crowded with Roman

229
The baby in the manger
Luke 2:7

The animals made snuffly noises around Mary and Joseph. Then suddenly there was the sound of a newborn baby crying. Mary's little boy was born. She wrapped him tightly in clean clothes to keep him warm and made a bed for him in the manger. She remembered that the angel had said his name would be Jesus.

soldiers and people tired from their journeys, all needing a place to stay. Mary was anxious to stop and rest but there was no room at the inn. 'We need to find somewhere soon,' she told Joseph. He found a place where there was straw on the floor and a manger filled with hay. Mary didn't mind the animals. She was happy to be off the dusty road and away from the eyes of the other travellers and the people of Bethlehem. She knew that soon her baby would come.

They shielded their eyes from the strange sight. 'Don't be afraid,' said an angel. 'I am bringing you good news! Jesus, your Saviour, has been born in Bethlehem. You will find him lying in a manger.'

230
Shepherds on the hillside
Luke 2:8–11

Out on the hills that night there were shepherds, watching over their sheep. Suddenly they were blinded by a bright light in the sky.

231
The song of the angels
Luke 2:12–14

As they looked they saw not one but hundreds of angels, lighting up the dark night sky. 'Glory to God who lives in heaven and peace to everyone who lives on earth,' they sang. The sound of the angels

was the most beautiful music the shepherds had ever heard. They listened until the angels had gone. Then they knew they must go to find the baby. They went into Bethlehem with the angels' song still echoing in their ears.

232
Visitors for Jesus
Luke 2:15–20

It was a dark but very starry night. The shepherds went through the streets until they found a baby lying in a manger, just as the angels had promised. Then they told Mary and Joseph about the angels and their message. In fact, they told everyone they met about the good news that Jesus was born! When they had gone, Mary wondered at all that had happened that night. She had given birth to her first baby, a baby promised to her by an angel, a baby who was God's son, the saviour of the world.

233
Saying thank you to God
Luke 2:21–34

Mary wanted to say thank you to
God for the gift of her baby son.
She went with Joseph to the temple
in Jerusalem to offer God two
pigeons in thanksgiving—a Jewish
custom. When they arrived an old
man named Simeon took the baby
from them and laughed with joy.
'God told me that I would see the
Saviour before I died! And here he is!'
he said.

234
Wise men from the east
Matthew 2:1

A new star appeared in the sky
when Jesus was born. Far away
in eastern lands, wise men, gazing
at the stars and studying their
positions, believed that it meant that
a new king had been born. They
decided to take him gifts and go to
worship him. They followed the star
to find the newborn king.

235
At the palace
Matthew 2:2

The wise men travelled a long way
from their home in the east until
they arrived in Jerusalem. They
went to the palace expecting to find
a baby king there. King Herod came
to meet them, wondering what their

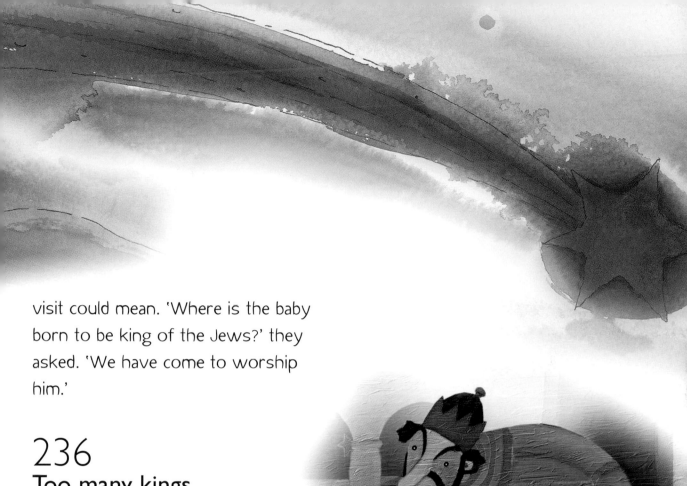

visit could mean. 'Where is the baby born to be king of the Jews?' they asked. 'We have come to worship him.'

236
Too many kings…
Matthew 2:3–5

King Herod was already king of Judea. But he was not a wise or a kind king; he was a cruel and jealous man. 'A baby?' he thought. 'There is room for only one king here!' So Herod asked his priests where the prophecies said that a king would be born. 'In Bethlehem,' came the answer.

237
The baby king
Matthew 2:4–8

King Herod listened to the news with growing anger. No king could be allowed to take his place! But he began to form a plan. He returned to greet his visitors, smiling sweetly. 'Go to Bethlehem,' he told them. 'I think you will find what you are looking for there. And when you find this special baby, this king of the Jews,' he said, 'please tell me so that I can worship him too...' He waved the wise men away—and then started to pace the floor.

238
Following the star
Matthew 2:9–10

The wise men mounted their camels and made their way to Bethlehem. 'Look!' said one. 'There's the star again!' They followed the star until it seemed to shine brightly over a house in Bethlehem. They unpacked their gifts and went to the house where they found Jesus with his mother, Mary.

239
Wise men worship
Matthew 2:11

Mary was surprised at her strange visitors. They had clearly travelled a long way to see her child. She looked at their rich clothing and wondered at the expensive gifts in their hands. Why had they come?

How did they know where to find Jesus? The wise men bowed down low and worshipped Mary's little boy. Then they offered the gifts they had brought from their treasure chests: gold, frankincense and myrrh. As they went out again into the starry night, Mary wondered about what it could all mean.

240
God's warning
Matthew 2:12

The wise men left the little family and rested before they returned to their homes in eastern lands. But that night, as they slept, God spoke to them in a dream and warned them not to go back the way they had come. Instead they were to make their journey back avoiding Jerusalem. King Herod was a dangerous man and could not be trusted. He was already planning

how he could harm the little boy they had come to worship. Jesus was not safe. So the wise men did not pass by King Herod's palace again; instead they went home another way.

241
Escape by night
Matthew 2:13–18

Mary and Joseph also slept badly that night. An angel appeared to Joseph in a dream and warned him about Herod too. 'Wake up!' he said, 'You must take Jesus and his mother and run away to Egypt! Herod will not rest until he has searched everywhere to find the child. He is already planning how he will have him killed!' So Joseph woke from his dream and told Mary to prepare for the journey. They did not wait till morning—they made their escape by night, taking Jesus to Egypt and safety. Not long afterwards Herod realised that the wise men were not coming back. Now he would not know where Jesus was or who he was. The king

was so angry that he calculated how old the child would be and then gave orders for every little boy under two years old to be killed! There was much weeping and wailing in Bethlehem because of King Herod's wickedness.

242
At home in Nazareth
Matthew 2:19–23

Jesus spent his early years in Egypt, being cared for by Mary and Joseph. When King Herod died, God spoke to Joseph in another dream and told him it was safe to take his family back to his own country. Mary and Joseph started the long journey back and made their home in Nazareth, in the area around Lake Galilee.

243
Jesus, the carpenter's son
Luke 2:41–43

Jesus grew up as other boys of his age did. Mary and Joseph took care of him and taught him how to love God and live by his laws. Most people knew him as Jesus, the carpenter's son. Every year, Mary and Joseph joined with many other people, travelling from Nazareth to Jerusalem for the Passover festival. Everyone looked forward to the singing and praying and parties, celebrating the time when God had led the Israelites out of Egypt in the time of Moses.

244
Where is Jesus?
Luke 2:44–45

When Jesus was twelve years old, Mary and Joseph went to Jerusalem as usual. It was only as they returned with their friends that they realised that neither of them had seen Jesus for a while. They thought he was with the other children but when they found that no one had seen him, they became very anxious. There was nothing else they could do; they turned around and left the others and walked back to Jerusalem.

Mary and Joseph walked the busy streets looking for Jesus. They searched for three days, becoming more anxious with every hour that passed. Where could he be? What could have happened? Then they went to the temple. There was Jesus, sitting talking with the religious leaders. 'Where have you been? We were so worried!' they said. 'I was here all the time, in my father's house,' Jesus told them. Other people may have thought he was the carpenter's son, but Jesus already knew who his father was.

245
Jesus is found
Luke 2:46–52

246
Elizabeth's son

Matthew 3:1–4

While Jesus was growing up into a man, Elizabeth's son, John, had grown up too. Now he was God's prophet. He was not afraid of what people thought of him. He lived in the desert and wore an itchy shirt of camel hair. He ate locusts and wild honey. He was there to prepare the people to welcome the man who would show them how to be God's friends; the one who had come to save them.

247
The prophet's message

Luke 3:3–14

'Come and tell God you are sorry for your sins,' said John. 'Stop doing bad things. Change your ways and learn to be kind. And don't just say you love God, show it by the good things you do. Don't be greedy—if you have enough food, share it with anyone who is hungry and if you have more clothes than you need, give some away to people who don't have enough. Be

honest in what you say and fair in everything you do; don't tell lies about people. Work hard and be content with what you have.'

248
Baptisms in the river
Matthew 3:7–12

People listened to John. Perhaps he was right—they should show God they were sorry for all the bad things they had done. They came and asked John to baptise them in the River Jordan. 'I baptise you with water to show that you want God to forgive you and wash you clean,' said John. 'But look out for someone coming soon who will baptise you with the Holy Spirit.'

249
The baptism of Jesus
Matthew 3:13–17

One day, Jesus came to the banks of the River Jordan and asked John to baptise him. John knew who he was immediately. 'But you have done nothing wrong!' John said. 'You don't need to say sorry. Instead, you should baptise me!' But Jesus asked John to baptise him anyway. When he did, all the people there saw the Holy Spirit come to him like a dove and heard God's voice say, 'This is my son. I love him and am pleased with what he has done today.'

250
The first nasty test
Matthew 4:1–4

It was time for Jesus to stop being the carpenter's son and to start showing people that he was God's son. So God's enemy, the devil, came to test him to see if he could be persuaded to break some of God's rules. Jesus went into the desert to pray. It was hot and dusty there. Jesus had nothing to eat for 40 days and 40 nights and he was very hungry. The devil said, 'If you really are God's son, you have power over nature. Why don't you turn these stones into bread? Then you can eat and you needn't be hungry any more.' Jesus replied, 'God's word says that people need much more than food to live. I trust God to give me all I need.'

251
The second nasty test
Matthew 4:5–7

Then the devil took Jesus out of the desert to the very top of the temple in Jerusalem. 'Look down,' said the devil. 'If you really are God's son, why don't you throw yourself down? Go on, I dare you! Hasn't God promised in his word that he

will send his angels to save you? Doesn't God say that angels will lift you up and take you down gently so that you will not even graze your foot on a stone? Go on, try it and see...' But Jesus said, 'Yes, God will save me, but his word also says that it is wrong to put him to the test. I will not do it.'

252
The last nasty test
Matthew 4:8–11

Jesus had not broken one of God's rules. Now the devil took him to the top of a very high mountain. From its peak Jesus could see how vast and beautiful the world was. It was breathtaking. 'Isn't it wonderful?' asked the devil. 'Wouldn't you like it to be yours, all yours? Well, it can be... I will give you all of this, the whole world, if you will only bow down and worship me. It's not much to ask in return, is it? What do you think?' But Jesus would not. 'No!' Jesus said. 'I will not! Get away from me! I will worship God and God alone.' Then the devil left Jesus and angels came to him. He had passed the tests set for him. He had not given in to the devil's temptations.

253
Water into wine

John 2:1–4

A wonderful wedding was happening in the village of Cana in Galilee. Everyone seemed to be invited—people from the village,

Mary, Jesus' mother, and Jesus and his friends too. There was a big party to celebrate the marriage of the young man and woman, a feast with lots of good things to eat and drink. After a while, Mary noticed that there was no more wine left. She was afraid the bride and groom would be embarrassed and the party spoiled. Perhaps Jesus could help? Mary knew that her son was special. So she told Jesus the problem. If he could do something, people would not know and everyone could continue to enjoy the celebrations.

254
The miracle at Cana
John 2:5–10

Jesus knew he could help but at first he was not sure it was the right time to do something that would make people take notice of him. He saw that there were six huge water pots standing nearby so that people could wash their hands in the water poured out from them. Jesus asked the servants to fill the pots to the top with clean water. 'Now offer some to the man in charge of the feast,' Jesus said. When the man

tasted it, it was no longer water, but the most delicious wine! It was a miracle, but only his mother, the servants and Jesus' friends knew what had happened.

255
No friends in Nazareth
Luke 4:14–30

It was time for Jesus to do the work God had sent him to do. Everywhere Jesus went in Galilee, people listened to him and were amazed at what he told them. Jesus talked about God as if he really knew him. He helped them to understand how much God loved them and cared about what happened in their lives. But Jesus had grown up in Nazareth. Here it was different. 'God has sent me to help the poor and to heal the deaf and blind,' Jesus said. 'God has sent me to show people how to live in a way that pleases him.' But the people there shook their heads. 'Surely we know Jesus?' they said. 'He is just the son of Joseph, the carpenter.'

out into deep water and do some fishing. 'We were out all last night,' Peter told Jesus. 'There was nothing there to catch. But we'll go if you want us to…' As soon as Peter and his companions put the nets into the water, they were filled with so many fish that the nets began to break!

257
Too many fish!
Luke 5:7–11

James and John were also in their boat on Lake Galilee. They saw what had happened and went to help Peter and Andrew—and soon the boats were full of silvery wriggling fish! Now both boats were in danger of sinking with the weight of the catch of fish. 'Follow me,' Jesus said. 'Then you will catch men and women instead of fish.' That day the four fishermen became the first of twelve men to become disciples of Jesus.

256
Fishing on Lake Galilee
Luke 5:1–6

Jesus needed some special friends to learn from him, some disciples to share his work. After he had taught the people for a while, he asked Simon Peter to push the boat

258
Friends in Capernaum

Mark 1:29–34, 38–42; 2:1–4

In Nazareth people could not believe that Jesus was the one sent by God to help them. But it was very different in Capernaum. Here Jesus was welcomed. Jesus had healed Peter's mother-in-law who had been in bed with a fever and many other people who had come to him for help. He had spent a few days in the nearby villages telling them about God's love and he had healed a man there who had leprosy. So by the time he returned to Capernaum, many people wanted to hear what Jesus had to say. Soon the house was overflowing! Outside the door were four men who wanted Jesus to help their friend who couldn't walk. They couldn't get through the door so they took the only other way. It was a bit unusual… They climbed the stairs outside the house that led to the roof. Then they worked at the mud and branches there until they had made a very large hole.

259
The hole in the roof
Mark 2:3–4

The men lowered their friend down carefully through the hole in the roof. Everyone looked up at the bits falling down on them. Some of the religious leaders there did not look happy. Other people were surprised—and some people thought it was rather funny. It was certainly the way to be noticed! The four friends were sure Jesus would do something to help their friend. They hoped that he would heal him completely. Jesus waited until the man on the mat was on the floor at his feet. Then he smiled at the man's friends. He knew exactly what they wanted.

260
Some very happy men
Mark 2:5–12

Jesus looked at the man on the mat. He knew everyone was waiting to see what would happen next. 'Come,' said Jesus, 'your sins are

forgiven.' No one in the room said anything—but Jesus knew what they were thinking. The religious leaders were shocked because they believed that only God could forgive sins. But they didn't know yet just who Jesus was. Then Jesus spoke again to the man. 'You can get to your feet now. You are healed. Pick up your mat and return to your home.' And the man did! He was very happy indeed—and so were his four friends!

261
Matthew becomes a disciple
Matthew 9:9–13

Matthew was at his work collecting taxes. He looked up at Jesus as he passed by. 'Come, Matthew—come and follow me!' Jesus said. Matthew did not hesitate. He got up and went. Then Matthew invited Jesus and his friends to dinner. All sorts of people were there—and the religious leaders did not approve of most of them! 'Why does Jesus mix with these bad people?' they asked. 'It's why I'm here,' said Jesus, 'to help the people who need me most.'

262
God's blessing
Matthew 5:1–12

Jesus soon attracted crowds of people. They were all keen to learn the things he knew about God. So Jesus sat down to teach them. Some of the things he said made them feel happy but there were some hard things too. 'God will bless you if you know you need his help. God will be there to comfort you if you are sad. God will satisfy you if you long for good things and he will be kind to you if you are kind to others. God will also bless you if people are unkind to you because you love God and do good things.'

263
Love and forgiveness
Matthew 5:38–48

'Love other people and forgive them if they hurt you. Treat them the way you would like people to treat you,' said Jesus. 'Don't hate someone or pay them back if they make you sad—treat them kindly and be generous to them instead. Love your enemies and pray for them, otherwise the people who love God are no different from everyone else. Be perfect, just as God is perfect.'

264
How to pray
Matthew 6:5–8

'Talk to God in secret, as if you are talking to a father who loves you and wants only the best things for you,' said Jesus. 'Don't pray just so that other people will be impressed. Tell God that you love him. Tell him what worries you. Be honest. God will answer. He knows what you need.'

265
The Lord's prayer
Matthew 6:9–13

'If you don't know how to start praying,' said Jesus, 'try this. "Our Father in heaven, your name is holy. Let peace and justice and kindness and all good things happen here on earth just as they do in heaven. Give us what we need to eat today and forgive us when we hurt others; help us to forgive people who hurt us. Help us when we are tempted to do things that are wrong. Keep us from getting into trouble or hurting other people."'

266
Trust God

Matthew 6:25–34

'Do you ever worry?' asked Jesus. 'Of course you do! But you don't need to—it doesn't change anything. Don't worry about what you will eat or what you will wear. Sparrows don't worry about how they'll find food. The flowers don't worry about the clothes they wear. God feeds the sparrows and makes the flowers beautiful and you are much more important to God than the birds or the flowers. Trust God and put him first and he will give you everything else you need.'

267
Be wise

Luke 6:46–48

Many people listened to the teaching of Jesus. But Jesus said it wasn't enough just to listen and nod. The important thing was to let his words change the way you acted.

268
Don't be foolish

Luke 6:49

'The person who ignores the things I have taught you and tries to take the easy way out will regret it,' said Jesus. 'That person will be like a man who builds their house on the sand. It will be much easier because there is less digging to do. But as soon as the storm comes and the wind howls, the walls will fall down and the roof will fall in. Everything he has worked for will be washed away. Don't be foolish, be wise. Listen to me and do what is right.'

'The person who acts on my words and does what is right is like a wise man who builds his house on a rock,' said Jesus. 'It may be hard work and it may take much longer, but when the storm comes and the wind howls, the wise man can sit back and know his house is safe and strong. Put what I say into practice and you will not be sorry. You will build your life on firm foundations.'

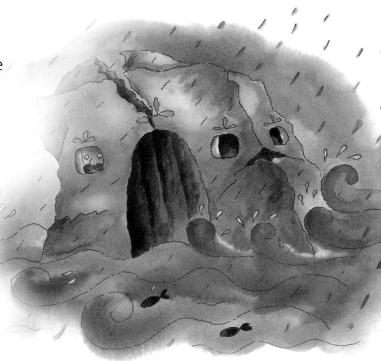

269
The soldier's servant

Matthew 8:5–9

When Jesus went to Capernaum, he met a Roman soldier who came to him asking for help. He was a good man who had built a synagogue for the local people. 'Please will you help? My servant is suffering in great pain,' the man said. Jesus was ready to go to help at once. 'I will go and heal him. Show me the way,' he said.

270
The soldier's faith

Matthew 8:10–13

The soldier shook his head. 'I don't deserve you to come to my house,' he said. 'I trust you to heal my servant. Just say he is healed and I know that he will be.' Jesus had never seen such faith before. 'God welcomes people everywhere to believe and you clearly trust God,' Jesus said. 'Go home now. Your servant is well again.' When the man returned to his house, his servant had been healed.

271
The widow's son

Luke 7:11–15

Jesus and his friends visited the town of Nain not long afterwards, followed by a crowd of people. At the gates of the town they met a funeral procession. The body of a young man was being carried away to be buried. His mother, a widow, was weeping for her only son. Jesus saw how sad she was. 'Don't cry,' he said to her. Jesus touched the dead man and immediately he was restored to life. The woman was overjoyed. But the people around were amazed. 'God has come to help his people,' they said.

272
Very precious treasure
Matthew 13:44

Jesus often told stories or parables to help people understand what he was saying. Sometimes the meaning was clear and other times they still needed help to understand. 'God's kingdom is like buried treasure in a field,' Jesus once said. 'When a man found this treasure, he sold everything he had to buy the field so that he could own the precious treasure. God's kingdom is precious like that. Do whatever you can to follow God's way. Nothing is more important. It's the best thing you will ever do.'

273
Very frightened disciples
Luke 8:22–23

One day Jesus told his disciples to cross to the other side of Lake Galilee. They all got into the fishing boat and Jesus put his head on a pillow to rest. He was very tired and was soon fast asleep. After a while the weather changed. The sky became dark and stormy and the gentle breeze became a wind that howled and tossed the boat high on the rough waves. All the disciples were frightened—even the fishermen among them!

274
Calm on the lake
Luke 8:24–25

Water began to slosh over the sides and into the boat. 'Master! Wake up!' the disciples shouted. 'Help us or we will drown!' Jesus woke up and realised quickly what was happening. He stood up and spoke to the wind and waves. 'Peace, be still!' he shouted over the sound of the wind. Almost as suddenly as it had begun, the storm had gone. The boat gently drifted on the water once more. 'Didn't you trust me?' Jesus asked the disciples. The disciples were amazed. How did Jesus do that?

275
People need Jesus' help
Luke 8:40–48

One day a man called Jairus came to ask Jesus for help. 'Please come to my house!' he begged. 'I have a daughter of twelve years old. She's my only child! But she is very ill—she is dying!' Jesus went quickly with Jairus, moving through the thick crowd of people. But there was in the crowd a woman who had been ill for twelve years. She needed Jesus' help too. If only she could touch him... Suddenly Jesus stopped. 'Who touched me?' he asked. Then he smiled at the woman. He knew what had happened. 'It's OK,' said Jesus. 'Your faith has healed you.'

276
Jairus' little girl

Luke 8:49–56

Someone else was pushing through the crowd, coming towards them. 'It's too late,' the man said to Jairus. 'I'm sorry, but your daughter has just died.' Jesus took Jairus by the arm. 'Don't worry; just trust me,' said Jesus. When they arrived at the house, Jesus sent everyone away except the girl's parents and three of his disciples. He knelt beside her bed. 'Get up, little girl,' Jesus said. Jairus' daughter opened her eyes and sat up. 'I think she's hungry,' smiled Jesus. 'She needs some food.' Her parents were very happy!

277
A secret visitor

John 3:1–17

The religious leaders had already decided that they did not like Jesus. But Nicodemus was not like the others. He was curious. He was interested. He was amazed at what Jesus taught about God. He wanted to know more but he didn't want everyone to know that he had spoken to Jesus. So Nicodemus came to see him in secret, at night. 'God sent me here to save people,' Jesus told him. 'God loves the world he has made so much that he has given his only son to save them. Anyone who believes in me will live for ever. But it is like being born a second time. Everything is new. You can start all over again.'

278
The woman at the well
John 4:4–30

As Jesus and his disciples passed through Samaria, Jesus sat by the well and rested while his friends went to find something to eat. It was the hottest part of the day but a woman had come to draw water from the well. 'Would you give me some water?' Jesus asked her. The woman was grumpy. 'I am surprised you are asking me—you Jews don't usually talk to Samaritans,' she replied. 'I know everything about you,' said Jesus. 'I can give you water that will stop you ever being thirsty again. I am the one you are waiting for, sent by God to save you.' The woman was amazed. She ran off to tell everyone she saw that Jesus was here.

279
Miracle on the mountain
Luke 9:12–17

Jesus had been talking to a crowd of over 5000 people. He had healed the people who were ill. But it was late. People were hungry and far from their homes. 'Where can we find food for everyone here?' Jesus asked his disciples. 'We have five pieces of bread and two fish,' said Andrew, 'but that won't go far.' The disciples told everyone to sit down while Jesus thanked God for the food. Jesus broke the bread and fish into pieces and gave them to the disciples to share among the people. When everyone had eaten, there were still twelve baskets of leftovers. It was a miracle!

280
Walking on water
Matthew 14:22–27

Later that same evening, Jesus told the disciples to go on without him across the lake while he stayed behind to pray for a while. Hours later, when the boat was a long way from the shore, the men in the boat saw someone coming towards them, walking on the water. 'Don't be afraid,' Jesus shouted. 'It's me!'

281
Peter meets Jesus
Matthew 14:28–31

Peter stood up in the boat. 'Lord, if it's really you,' he said, 'let me come to you across the lake.' Then Peter stepped out on to the water and started to walk towards Jesus. But as soon as the wind blew around him, Peter took his eyes off Jesus. Suddenly he started to sink into the waves. Jesus caught his hand and helped him back into the boat. 'Why were you afraid, Peter?' Jesus asked. 'Didn't you trust me?'

282
The man who couldn't hear
Mark 7:32–37

As Jesus visited the towns around Lake Galilee, some people came to him with a man who was completely deaf. As he could not hear, he could not speak either. 'Please, can you help him?' they asked Jesus. Jesus took the man away from his friends to a quiet place. Then Jesus touched the man's ears and his tongue and healed him. The man returned to his friends able to speak and hear. It was another miracle!

283
Who is my neighbour?
Luke 10:25–29

A man once asked Jesus how he could best show God that he loved him. 'What do the scriptures teach you?' asked Jesus. 'I know I must love God with all my heart and soul and strength—with every bit of me,' said the man. 'And I must love my neighbour as much as I love myself. But who exactly is my neighbour?' Jesus answered him by telling him a story about a good Samaritan.

284
The good Samaritan
Luke 10:30–37

'A man was travelling from Jerusalem to Jericho,' said Jesus, 'when he was attacked by robbers. They took everything he had and left him for dead. After a while, a priest came by—but he walked past him and went on his way; he would not touch him. Then a Levite came along. He crossed over so he wouldn't get too close as the man lay wounded on the road. The wounded man felt the hot sun beat down on him and was sure that he would die. But a little later a Samaritan came along the road. Everyone knows that Israelites and Samaritans don't speak to each other. But the Samaritan stopped to help. He bathed and bandaged the man's wounds. Then he helped him on to his own donkey and took him to an inn where he paid for the man to be looked after till he was well. Now, who do you think was a good neighbour to the man who was hurt?' The man replied, 'The one who was kind to him.' Jesus said, 'Now go and do the same.'

knew their sheep and the sheep knew the shepherd's voice. 'You are like my sheep,' said Jesus one day. 'I am like a good shepherd. I know you all by your name, and there is nothing I wouldn't do to take care of you. I would even die to save you.'

285
The good shepherd
John 10:11–15

The land that Jesus lived in had many sheep on the hillsides. A stranger might have thought they all looked just the same. But the shepherds

286
The lost sheep
Luke 15:3–7

'Imagine you own 100 sheep,' said Jesus. 'One day you find that there are only 99. What do you do? I will tell you. You search everywhere for that little lost sheep until you find him. You cannot rest till you can carry him home again on your shoulders! God's love is like that. He cares about everyone, especially the one that is lost and alone.'

287
The lost son
Luke 15:11–19

'A man once had two sons.' Jesus was telling another of his stories. 'The younger son asked for his inheritance, left home and had soon spent it all. He took a job looking after pigs but was so hungry that he wanted to eat the pigs' food! He decided to ask his father if he could work as a servant on his farm. But would his father take him back?'

288
The loving father
Luke 15:20–32

'The boy's father had been watching and waiting for him. "Father," the boy said, "I've been so silly and I am really sorry…" But his father threw his arms around him and hugged him. "Let's celebrate!" he said. "My son was lost, but now he's found!" God loves you all,' said Jesus. 'He is always ready to forgive your mistakes.'

289
Treasures in heaven
Luke 12:16–20, 33–34

'Try not to be greedy,' Jesus said. 'Life is more important than the things money can buy.' Then he told a story. 'Once there was a rich farmer who had a very good harvest. He didn't have enough room to store all his crops, so he pulled down his barns and built new bigger, better barns. "What a lucky man I am!" he thought. He planned to relax and enjoy life. But that night, he died. His wealth was no good to him any more. So,' said Jesus, 'don't store your treasure here on earth where moths can eat it and robbers steal it. Share what you have, and store up treasure in heaven.'

a woman there who had been bent over for 18 years so that she could not straighten up at all. Jesus touched her and healed her. 'You are free now,' he said. Then the woman found she could stand up straight— she was healed! 'Thank you, God! Thank you!' she said. All the people were happy for the woman and loved Jesus for healing her. But the leader of the synagogue was cross. Jesus had broken the rules; he had healed someone on the sabbath day.

290
Healed on the sabbath day
Luke 13:10–17

Jesus often went to the synagogue to teach people on the sabbath day when the Jewish people worshipped God. One day he met

291
Ten desperate men
Luke 17:11–14

As Jesus came into a village one day, he saw ten men huddled together, waiting for him. Jesus knew they had a skin disease called leprosy. They were outcasts, not allowed to live with their families in case they became ill too. 'Help us, Lord!' they cried. 'You can go home,' said Jesus. 'I have healed you.'

292
The man who came back
Luke 17:14–19

The men could hardly believe it! They showed each other their smooth, healthy skin and hurried home. But one man ran after Jesus. 'Thank you, Lord, for making me well!' he said. Jesus smiled at the man. 'You trusted me to help you and you are healed,' he said. But Jesus looked sadly into the distance. Why did the others not say thank you too?

293
Mary and Martha

Luke 10:38–42

Jesus was very good friends with a man named Lazarus and his sisters, Martha and Mary, who lived in a village called Bethany. One day Jesus and his disciples stopped at their house. 'Come in, come in!' said Martha. She made her guests comfortable and then hurried into the kitchen to prepare food and drinks for them all. But while Martha was being busy in the kitchen, Mary sat with their guests and listened to all Jesus was telling them about God. 'Tell Mary to come and help me!' Martha called out to Jesus. But

Jesus shook his head. 'Mary is fine here with me,' he said. 'You mustn't be so anxious, Martha. Sometimes it's better to spend time with people while you can.'

294
Lazarus is very ill

John 11:1–6, 17–33

Some time later, someone came to tell Jesus that Lazarus was very ill. Jesus wanted to go to be with his friend, but he was busy helping other people some distance away. When he arrived at their house a few days later, Martha met Jesus on the road. She told him that Lazarus had died and been buried four days before. 'Lord, if you had been here,

I know my brother would still be alive,' she said. Her eyes were wet with tears. 'But I know you are God's son. God will give you whatever you ask.'

295
Jesus prays for Lazarus
John 11:31–46

Mary and all the friends who had come to comfort her came out to join Jesus. They went together to the tomb where Lazarus had been buried. Jesus was so sad that he cried with them for his friend. But then Jesus prayed, 'Father, we need a miracle now so that everyone here will know that you have sent me.' Jesus turned and said, 'Lazarus! Come out!' And while everyone watched, Lazarus walked out from the tomb in his grave clothes—very much alive! Many of the people who were there realised that only God's son could make

this happen. But some went to the religious leaders and began to stir up trouble for Jesus.

296
Jesus blesses children
Mark 10:13–16

Among the crowds of people who gathered wherever Jesus went were children. Mothers brought them so Jesus could bless them. Jesus always had time for children. He laughed with them and told them stories. They loved to be wherever he was. 'My kingdom is made up of people like these children,' Jesus said. 'Their faith is simple. They are ready to love and trust God with all their hearts.'

297
What do you love most?

Mark 10:17–25

A rich young man once asked Jesus, 'What do I have to do to live in heaven?' Jesus knew the man had a good heart, but there was one thing wrong. 'Love God more than you love your money,' Jesus answered. 'Give it away to the poor. They need it and you have more than enough.' Then the man was very sad. He turned and walked away. He was very rich and he knew that he could not do as Jesus asked. His money seemed more important.

298
The blind beggar

Luke 18:35–38

Jesus was travelling through Jericho and the streets were lined with people. 'What's all the noise about?' a blind beggar asked. He was sitting by the roadside, hoping people would give him money. Someone told him that Jesus was passing by. The blind man had heard all about Jesus. He knew that Jesus had healed people like him. Perhaps Jesus would help him too? Maybe Jesus would do more than put money in his begging bowl. Could Jesus even give him eyes that could see? 'Jesus, son of David, have mercy on me!' he shouted at the top of his voice.

299
The blind man sees!

Luke 18:39–43

'Be quiet!' people shouted back. 'Jesus is busy!' But the blind beggar kept trying to get Jesus' attention. Jesus stopped. 'What do you want me to do for you?' he asked. 'I want to see!' the blind man said. 'Your faith has made you well,' Jesus replied. 'Go now: you can see!' The blind beggar had what he wanted— and he joined the people who followed Jesus.

300
The little tax collector

Luke 19:1–4

Elbow to elbow, the streets were packed as Jesus went through Jericho. And no one was going to make room for Zacchaeus, the rich tax collector. He was a cheat! So Zacchaeus climbed up a fig tree so that he could see Jesus as he passed by. But Jesus could see Zacchaeus too. He stopped right under the tree.

301
Zaccheus meets Jesus
Luke 19:5–10

'Zaccheus, I'd like to visit your house today,' Jesus said, smiling up at him through the branches. All the people around Jesus were shocked. Why would Jesus take notice of a man like Zaccheus? Why would he be kind to him? But Zaccheus changed when he met Jesus. 'I'm going to give half my money to the poor,' he said. 'I won't cheat anyone again. I will even pay back what I have stolen—and much more too!' Then Jesus told everyone, 'I came to find people, like Zaccheus, who need God's help. This is why I am here.'

302
Who are the good people?
Matthew 25:31–40

'One day God will judge everyone according to how they have lived,' Jesus told his disciples. 'The good people will be separated from the bad. "You have done well," God will say to some. "When I was hungry, you gave me food. When I needed clothes, you shared yours with me. When I was in prison or in hospital, you visited me." The good people will ask, "But when did we do these things?" God will answer, "Whenever you were kind to someone who needed help, you did it for me."'

303
Who are the bad people?
Matthew 25:41–46

Then Jesus said, 'God will say to the others, "Go away from me! You would not help when I was cold and hungry; or visit when I was sad in prison and lonely in hospital." "But when did we do these things?" they will say. He will answer, "Whenever you saw someone who needed help and only had time for yourselves, you were turning your back on me."'

304
A present for Jesus
John 12:1–8

When Jesus went to visit his friends, Lazarus, Martha and Mary, he had a surprise. The men were sitting around the table when Mary came in with a bottle of expensive perfume. Mary knelt by Jesus' feet and washed them with the perfume. The whole room was filled with the wonderful scent. Then she dried Jesus' feet with her long hair. 'What a waste!' grumbled Judas. 'We could have sold the perfume and given the money to the poor!' But Jesus shook his head and smiled at Mary. 'No, I will not be here much longer and Mary has done something kind and generous.'

305
Jesus rides a donkey
John 12:12–19

People were beginning to prepare for the Passover feast. Jesus asked his disciples to borrow a donkey so that he could ride into Jerusalem. When the people saw him, they remembered that long ago, a prophet had written that their king would ride on a donkey, not a war horse. Soon they were waving branches from palm trees and cheering. 'God bless Jesus!' they shouted. 'Here comes King Jesus!' The religious leaders frowned and muttered. They didn't like it at all.

said. Now the religious leaders were very angry. 'This cannot go on,' they whispered. 'We must find a way to stop Jesus for ever.'

306
Lots of noise in the temple
Mark 11:15–18

When Jesus went to the temple to pray, he saw many people selling animals for offerings. He saw money-changers cheating the visitors. 'God's house is a place for love and kindness and for people to pray,' Jesus shouted. Then he turned over their tables. 'It's not a place for cheating and stealing!' he

307
A very generous woman
Mark 12:41–44

People came to the temple with money for the poor. 'Look how much that woman loves God,' Jesus said to his friends. 'That widow has given two copper coins for God's work. She has very little but she has given more than everyone else. They gave what they had left over; she gave God everything that she had.'

308
Plots against Jesus
Matthew 26:3–5

'Jesus must go!' the priests and religious leaders said. 'He cannot continue teaching people about God. People won't listen to us any more.' But they were also afraid. Everyone loved Jesus. They knew there would be a riot if they arrested Jesus. They needed one of his friends to betray him so they could do it secretly... Jesus knew they were plotting. 'I will not be with you much longer,' Jesus told his disciples.

309
The importance of love
John 13:5–20

It was time to celebrate the Passover feast together. Jesus and his disciples met in the upstairs room of a house in Jerusalem. Before they sat down to eat together, Jesus filled a basin with water and began

to wash their dusty feet. It was usually the job of a servant. 'Follow my example,' Jesus told them. 'Don't argue about who is the most important among you. Instead learn to take care of each other. Do things for others that are kind and good and the world will know that you love me.'

310
Who will betray Jesus?
John 13:21–25

As they sat at the table, Jesus was surrounded by his twelve disciples for the last time. 'You are all my friends but I know that one of you will betray me to my enemies,' he told them. The disciples looked at each other. They had all seen the people Jesus had healed. They had heard the stories Jesus had told them about God's love. Who could do such a thing? 'Who is it, Lord?' they asked. Jesus wouldn't tell them but when he looked at Judas, Judas looked nervously at his feet.

311
Who will deny Jesus?
John 13:31–38

'I want you to love each other in the same way that I have loved you,' Jesus said to them. 'You know that I would do anything you ask, Lord!' said Peter quickly. 'I would even die for you!' Jesus smiled back sadly. 'Oh, Peter, before the cock crows at dawn tomorrow, you will have said three times that you do not even know me.' Jesus told his friends that soon he would be going away—and this time they could not follow him. 'Don't be afraid,' Jesus said. 'I am going to prepare a place for you in God's house.'

189

312
Judas creeps away
John 13:27–30

Jesus turned to Judas and said, 'Do what you have to do now, but go quickly.' The other disciples thought that Judas was going to give money to the poor. He had 30 silver coins in his pocket. It was not for the poor—it was the money Judas had been given to take the religious leaders to Jesus. Judas knew the quiet places that Jesus went to pray.

313
A house with many rooms
John 14:1–6

'Don't be afraid—trust God. Soon I will go to my father's house where there are many rooms, and I will make a place ready for you,' Jesus said. 'How will we get there, Lord?' Thomas asked. 'I am the way, the truth and the life. I am the bridge between you and God,' Jesus answered. 'If you know me, you also know God himself. Trust me and you will have a place in heaven.'

314
The last supper

Mark 14:22–26

Jesus knew that this would be the last meal he ate with his disciples before his death. He knew that Judas was even now with his enemies getting ready to come and arrest him. Jesus did not have much more time with his friends but even now they did not understand that something very bad was going to happen soon. In just a few hours he would be taken away from them and terrible things would happen. Jesus broke some bread and shared it with them. 'Eat this,' he said. 'This is my body which is broken for you.' Then Jesus took a cup of wine and said, 'Drink this. This is my blood which will be spilled for you.' Then they sang a song together before leaving to go out to the Mount of Olives to pray.

315
Praying in the garden
Matthew 26:36–38

Jesus led his eleven disciples to a garden called Gethsemane. Silver-grey olive trees lit by the full moon surrounded them. It was very quiet. Jesus said to Peter, James and John, 'I feel very sad and lonely tonight. Please stay close by and pray with me.' Then Jesus went a little further so that he could be alone with God but knowing that his friends were near. Then Jesus prayed to his father.

316
Jesus is alone
Matthew 26:39–41

'Father God,' Jesus prayed. 'I know that there is much sadness and suffering to come. I know that soon I must die. But please, if there is any other way to save the people that you love, the people that I love, then help me now. If not, then I want to do whatever you want. Please help me to do it bravely.' Jesus got up from his knees and returned to where Peter, James and John were praying. But he found that they were not praying at all—they had fallen asleep! Jesus felt even more alone. He woke his friends. 'Could you not pray with me even for an hour?' he asked them. 'I know you want to help me. Please keep watch and pray.'

317
Sleeping friends
Matthew 26:42–46

Jesus knew he had very little time left. Clouds were moving across the moon. He knelt and prayed again. 'Please, Father God, help me now. If it is not possible for what happens next just to go away; if I must take the next difficult step, I know this is the right thing to do. I want what you want.' Then Jesus went again to his disciples. Again he found them sleeping! They were just too tired. They couldn't stay awake. Jesus woke them again and then went to pray a third time. Each time he asked for strength because he knew that only he could do the job that lay ahead of him. This is what he had been born to do. Then Jesus saw that his friends were asleep once more. He knew that it was too late. Even now there were sounds in the trees; the quiet of the garden was broken.

318
Judas and the armed guards
Matthew 26:47–50

The disciples awoke to confusion. A band of men armed with swords and clubs sent by the religious leaders was coming towards them. And there, right at the front, coming to greet Jesus with a kiss, was Judas. It was not the kiss of friendship. Judas was giving a sign so the men would know whom to arrest. 'I know why you are here,' Jesus said to Judas. 'Go ahead. I am ready.'

319
Jesus is a prisoner!
Mark 14:48–50

The crowd of armed men grabbed
Jesus and arrested him. The disciples
were terrified. They couldn't believe
what was happening. They didn't
know what to do. 'Why do you
need swords and clubs?' Jesus
asked the men. 'Did you think I
was leading a rebellion? Every day
I have been in the temple or with
the people. You could have come
at any time but you didn't arrest
me then!' But Jesus knew why
they had not come when he was
with the people who loved him. He
knew the crowds would not have
let this happen. As the men began to
push Jesus through the garden, his
friends, afraid that the soldiers had
also come for them, ran away into
the darkness and left him.

320
'Are you the son of God?'
Matthew 26:57–68

Peter waited until the men had gone
ahead and then followed, keeping
to the shadows so he could not be
seen. The guards marched Jesus
away to the house of Caiaphas, the
high priest. The religious leaders
had gathered to put Jesus on trial.
'Tell us whether you are the Christ,
the son of God,' they demanded.
Jesus simply said, 'You have said it
yourself.' Caiaphas was very angry.
How could this man claim to be God?
'This is blasphemy!' he said. 'This
is a crime worthy of death. Now
we have the evidence we need to
condemn him!' Then the men spat at
Jesus and hit him. All this time, Peter
was waiting outside in the shadows
to see what would happen.

321
Peter is ashamed
Matthew 26:69–75

A servant girl was staring at Peter. 'Aren't you a friend of that man in there?' she asked him. 'No!' said Peter. 'I don't know what you mean.' Then another girl came and accused him too. 'He was with Jesus!' she said. 'No, you're wrong! I don't know the man,' Peter said. Then someone else said he had the same accent as Jesus. Peter denied it a third time. Then he heard the cock crow... and remembered what Jesus had said. Peter cried with shame.

322
A bad end for Judas
Matthew 27:1–5

Only Pontius Pilate, the Roman governor, could decide if someone should die. The religious leaders took Jesus to him. 'This man is a troublemaker!' the chief priests told

Pilate. When Judas saw what was happening, he was sorry. 'Here—take your money. I have done a terrible thing. This man is innocent!' When the religious leaders would not take back the money, Judas threw it into the temple. Then he went away and killed himself.

323
Jesus on trial
Matthew 27:11–26

Pilate could tell Jesus was innocent but he didn't want more trouble. Outside, a bloodthirsty crowd, bribed by the religious leaders, was shouting, 'Crucify him!' They looked up at Pontius Pilate. He knew Jesus had done nothing wrong, but he was afraid. 'I can set a prisoner free as it is Passover,' he said. 'Barabbas, the murderer? Or the man you call your king—Jesus from Nazareth? Who do you want?' 'Free Barabbas!' they shouted. 'Then what about Jesus?' 'Crucify him!' they shouted.

324
The crown of thorns
Matthew 27:27–31

It was a Friday morning when the Roman soldiers took Jesus away. They dressed him in a scarlet robe and put a stick in his hand. 'You're supposed to be a king, aren't you?' they said, laughing. 'You need a crown!' The soldiers beat him and pushed a crown of sharp thorns on to his head.

325
The way to the cross
Mark 15:20–22

The cruel soldiers led Jesus away to the place where the Romans crucified their prisoners. Jesus had to carry on his shoulders the heavy piece of wood that would become part of the cross he would die on. Jesus, tired and weak from the beating, kept stumbling and falling down. The soldiers pulled a man out of the crowd and made him carry the wood the rest of the way. The man's name was Simon.

326
Two thieves
Luke 23: 32–43

The soldiers nailed Jesus to the piece of wood and hung the cross up high between two thieves. 'Forgive them, Father,' said Jesus, even in his pain. One of the other crucified men called out to Jesus. 'You saved other people: why don't you save yourself?' But the other man said, 'Leave him alone! We deserve our punishment, but he does not. Please, Jesus, remember me.' Jesus answered, 'Today you will be with me in heaven.'

327
Jesus takes care of Mary
John 19:26–27

Long hours passed while Jesus was on the cross. Some people were nearby weeping for him. Jesus saw his mother with one of his disciples. 'Mother!' Jesus said. 'Treat John as your son now.' Then he looked at John and said, 'Look after Mary. Take care of her as if she were your own mother.' John was very sad to see his friend suffering. He comforted Mary as they both stood waiting, knowing that soon Jesus would die.

328
A cruel death
Matthew 27:50–54

Although it was still daytime, the sky became very dark. Jesus felt very alone. He thought that even God, his Father, had deserted him. But Jesus knew that he was dying not because of anything he had done wrong, but in the place of all the people in the world who had ever done things wrong and who would ever do bad things in the future. Then Jesus died.

tomb which was in a garden near the cross. They wound a clean linen sheet around his body with special spices. Then they rolled a large stone against the entrance to close it tightly. Some of the women who were friends of Jesus came to see where he was buried.

329
A sad Friday evening
Mark 15:42–46

There was a rich man from Arimathea called Joseph who had been one of Jesus' friends. He went to Pilate and asked if he could take down Jesus' body from the cross and bury him in his own tomb before the sabbath day. The soldiers put a sword in Jesus' side to make sure Jesus was dead before they would release the body.

330
Buried in a cave
John 19:38–42

Joseph and Nicodemus, the man who had come to Jesus secretly, took Jesus' body and placed it in a

331
The empty tomb
John 19:42—20:1

The next day was the sabbath, a special day of rest. So it was early on Sunday morning, while it was still dark, that Mary Magdalene came to visit the place where she had seen Jesus buried. But the large stone had been rolled away. When she peeped inside, the tomb was empty!

332
Jesus is alive!

John 20:1–18

Mary went to tell Peter and John that Jesus' body was not there and they ran to the tomb to see for themselves. What could this mean? They left Mary weeping in the garden. Then angels came and asked Mary why she was crying. 'Someone has taken Jesus away,' she wept. Then she realised someone else was there. Mary thought it was the gardener until the man spoke her name. Mary knew that voice. It was Jesus! He was not dead any more. Jesus was alive and he was here talking to her! Mary could not wait to tell his friends.

333
Inside a locked room
John 20:19–23

That same day, some of the disciples were together in a room with the doors locked. They were very sad because Jesus had died. They were also still afraid that soldiers would arrest them too. Suddenly, everything changed. They were no longer alone. Jesus was there in the room with them! 'You're alive!' they shouted. Then Jesus showed them the marks where the nails had hurt him. Now they understood that he had died—but he had risen from the dead. It was another miracle.

334
The road to Emmaus
Luke 24:13–35

Two of the disciples were travelling to Emmaus on the same Sunday. They were talking to each other about the events of the past few days—how Jesus had been arrested and crucified, but then had been seen again alive after his burial. While they were walking, someone joined them. The man asked them what they were discussing and they told him. Then the stranger began to tell them how the scriptures they had known from childhood had told them that one day all these things would take

place. Now it had all happened in their lifetime to someone they knew and they had seen it for themselves. When they arrived at Emmaus, they invited the man to eat with them. As soon as he broke the bread and asked God to bless it, they realised that this was no stranger at all—it was Jesus!

335
Doubting Thomas
John 20:24–29

Thomas had not been with the other disciples when Jesus had come into the locked room. Now he could not believe that Jesus was alive. 'I must see him with my own eyes,' he said. Eight days later, Jesus appeared again in the same way. 'Look at the nail marks, Thomas,' Jesus said. 'Put your hands here in the wound at my side.' Thomas fell to his knees. It really was Jesus!

net on the right side of the boat!'
When Peter did, the net was filled
with fish!

337
Breakfast with Jesus
John 21:7–11

Peter knew that the man on the
shore must be Jesus. He jumped
into the water and left his friends
to bring in the catch of fish while
he swam to shore. There was a fire
and warm bread waiting for them.
'Bring some of the fish you've
caught,' Jesus said. 'Let's have
breakfast together.' The disciples
dragged in the heavy net. They had
caught 153 fish!

336
Night fishing
on Lake Galilee
John 21:1–6

'Let's go fishing,' Peter said to his
friends one evening. Seven of the
disciples went out that night but
after many hours on Lake Galilee,
they hadn't caught anything. It was
nearly dawn when a man called to
them from the shore. 'Throw your

338
Peter is forgiven
John 21:15–17

Jesus knew that Peter was still
sad. Peter couldn't forget that, after
Jesus had been arrested, he had told

people he was not his friend not just once but three times. He still felt ashamed that he had let Jesus down, and needed to be able to tell Jesus that he was sorry. But Jesus knew that. Jesus walked along the shore with Peter. Then Jesus asked Peter the same question three times, just as Peter had denied him three times. 'Peter, do you love me more than the others do?' he asked. 'Yes, I do, Lord! You know I do!' Then Jesus gave Peter a huge task. 'Peter, I have a special job for you to do,' Jesus said. 'I want you to look after my followers.'

Jesus was ready to return to his Father in heaven. 'I must go very soon,' he told his friends. 'But don't be afraid, I will not leave you alone. Wait in Jerusalem and the Holy Spirit will come to you. It will be as if I were always there to help you.' Then suddenly Jesus was gone. Two angels appeared. 'Don't look for Jesus on earth any more,' they said. 'He is in heaven. But one day he will come back.'

339
Jesus goes to heaven
Acts 1:1–11

More than a month had passed since Jesus had risen from the dead. He had spent time with his friends and it had been very special. But now

340
A new disciple
Acts 1:12–26

Jesus' friends gathered in Jerusalem to pray together. All the disciples were there except Judas, but Mary, Jesus' mother, and many other

341
The Holy Spirit comes
Acts 2:1—4

People had come from all over the world to celebrate the harvest festival known as Pentecost. The city was buzzing with people speaking different languages. Jesus' friends were together in a house in Jerusalem for the Pentecost celebrations. Suddenly the Holy Spirit came to them. They heard a sound like a rushing wind and saw what looked like tongues of fire on each person. They realised that the Holy Spirit had given them strength to do the good things that Jesus wanted them to do. It was as if Jesus was there with them all the time wherever they went. They would never feel alone.

men and women who had been his friends were there too—about 120 people. 'We need someone to take Judas' place,' said Peter. 'We must pray that God will help us choose the right person.' God helped them to choose Matthias, who had been with them since the day Jesus was baptised. He became the twelfth disciple.

to be forgiven. Come now and tell him that you are sorry and you can be his friend too.' About 3000 people became Christians that day.

343
The man who needed help
Acts 3:1–10

A man who could not walk sat by one of the temple gates begging day after day. Peter and John saw him there as they went to the temple to pray. 'Do you have any money?' the man asked them. 'Can you spare any coins?' Peter smiled at the man. 'I don't have any money I can share with you,' Peter said, 'but with Jesus' help, I can offer you a much

342
Many new believers!
Acts 2:14–36

Peter had been afraid once to tell people that Jesus was his friend. But now he was not only able to stand up and speak to a huge crowd, he could speak in languages he had never learned. They all could! The house had been filled with sound and now a crowd had gathered outside. Peter went out to talk to them. 'Do you remember Jesus?' he asked. 'You crucified him! But God gave him new life—and we saw him and talked with him ourselves. We are witnesses of his resurrection! Now Jesus will forgive anyone who believes he is God's son and wants

greater gift.
I can help you
to walk.' Then by
the power of the Holy
Spirit the man was healed!
He got to his feet and thanked
God for healing him. Then he jumped
up and down with joy. Peter and
John watched the man and then
saw others turning to look at him in
surprise.

344
The Holy Spirit's power
Acts 4:1–4

Everyone who went to the temple
knew the man who had been
healed. They had seen him begging
every day. So now they saw that a
miracle had happened. A man who
could not walk was walking. But
how? Everyone was amazed. 'Why
are you surprised?' Peter asked
them. 'You allowed Pilate to crucify
Jesus. You saw that he died and

was buried. But God raised him to
new life. That was a miracle and so
is this. A paralysed man can walk
because of the power of the Holy
Spirit.' The temple guards didn't like
this at all. They grabbed Peter and
John and threw them into prison.

345
Prisoners for God
Acts 4:5–20

Peter and John were questioned the next morning. 'How did you heal this man?' The Holy Spirit helped Peter to answer, just as Jesus had promised. 'Jesus healed him. And only Jesus can heal and forgive and save any of us. You have seen this miracle for yourselves.' The religious leaders knew they could not keep Peter and John in prison, because many people had already seen that it was true. 'OK, we will let you go—but only if you promise not to keep talking about Jesus and his teaching.'

Peter and John could not promise. 'We cannot help telling everyone about Jesus!' they said. 'Who do you think we should obey—you or God himself?'

346
Peter and John are free
Acts 4:4, 21–35

There were now about 5000 believers in Jerusalem, sharing with each other everything they owned, living the way that Jesus had taught them. 'Help us not to be afraid as we tell people about you, Lord,' they prayed. 'Let people see the miracles done in your name and know that you are the true and living God so that they can know you for themselves.'

347
The first Christian martyr
Acts 6:1—7:60

The twelve disciples chose seven men to help them look after people who were ill or poor. Stephen was one of them. God blessed Stephen so that he was able to heal many people and speak bravely about Jesus. Many people became Christians because they saw that Stephen was kind and loving like Jesus. But the religious leaders hated him. They arranged for him to be stoned to death.

348
Saul hates Christians
Acts 8:1–3

Saul believed in God. He was a very religious man, but he was sure that the Christians were wrong about Jesus and hated all that they said and did. So when Stephen was killed, Saul looked on, pleased at what had happened. Then he went from house to house, looking for all the believers and throwing them into prison. He would not rest until they were all stopped from telling people about Jesus.

349
Philip goes to Samaria
Acts 8:4–8

The new Christians had asked for God's help. Now they needed it more than ever. Those who were

not imprisoned left Jerusalem, but wherever they went, they told people about Jesus. Philip went to Samaria and healed people who were disabled and told them how to love God and follow Jesus. There were many happy people in Samaria while Philip was there.

350
The man in the chariot
Acts 8:26–38

While Philip was praying, God told him to go down to the road between Jerusalem and Gaza. Philip did not know why, but when he got there he met an important man from Ethiopia sitting in a chariot and reading aloud from one of the prophecies about Jesus. 'Do you understand what you are reading?' Philip asked. 'No. Please help me,' the man replied. So Philip told him that God had sent Jesus, his son, to die on a cross. Anyone who trusted him could be forgiven for all the wrong things they had done. The man did trust Jesus. He asked Philip to baptise him!

351
Jesus talks to Saul
Acts 9:3–8

Saul was still trying to find Christians and put them in prison. He was travelling with friends to Damascus when suddenly he was blinded by a light from heaven. 'Saul, why are you persecuting me?' came a voice. 'Who are you?' asked Saul, who couldn't see who was speaking. 'I am Jesus,' came the answer. 'Listen to me. I have an important job for you to do.' Saul's friends also heard the voice and saw no one. They had to lead Saul to Damascus because he could not see.

352
Cornelius sees an angel
Acts 10:1–8

Cornelius was a Roman soldier from the Italian regiment. He had learned about God while working in Israel. Cornelius and his family loved God, gave generously to people in need and prayed often. So when an angel appeared one day with a message for him, Cornelius listened. 'God has heard your prayers and seen the good things you do,' said the angel. 'Now, find Peter who is in a house by the sea in Joppa and he will teach you more.'

353
Peter's rooftop vision
Acts 10:9–20

Meanwhile, Peter was praying on the roof of the house in Joppa. Peter was hungry and while he prayed, he had a vision. He saw in the vision that God was offering him all kinds of birds and animals to eat, including those normally forbidden to Jewish men and women. 'But these animals aren't clean, Lord,' Peter said. 'I mustn't eat them.' God replied, 'Once that was true, but now I have made them clean and holy.' The same thing happened three times before all the animals disappeared again. While Peter was wondering what the vision could mean, he heard someone call to him from the gate of the house. Then the Holy Spirit told Peter to go with the men.

354
Peter meets Cornelius
Acts 10:24–33

The men at the gate explained that they had come from Cornelius. The next day Peter went with them

to the soldier's house. Then Peter understood his strange vision. Peter and his friends had always believed that they were God's holy chosen people and God's offer of new life was only for them. God was telling him that Jesus had come to make everyone welcome in God's kingdom—even Roman soldiers and their families. 'God has no favourites,' Peter told the people gathered in the house. Then the Holy Spirit came to Cornelius and all the people there and they were baptised as Christians.

355
Passover in prison
Acts 12:1–6

Herod Agrippa was now king in Judea. He had James, John's brother, put to death. Then he put Peter in prison. Herod planned to give Peter a public trial before killing him too! So Peter spent Passover in chains in a dark cell with a guard on either side of him and two more soldiers guarding the door. He was very sad at what had happened to James; he also knew that Herod would probably put him to death the next day or soon afterwards.

356
Friends pray for Peter
Acts 12:5–10

But Peter was not alone. His friends all knew what had happened and they had gathered in the house of John Mark's mother. They prayed for their friend into the late hours of the night, asking God to help him and to stop him from being afraid. God answered their prayers in a very unexpected way. While they were praying, God sent an angel into the prison to wake the sleeping Peter. 'Quick, get up,' said the angel. As Peter stood up, the chains fell from his wrists, freeing him from the guards beside him. 'Get dressed and put on your sandals,' said the

angel. So Peter got ready to go out into the night, still amazed at what was happening. 'Now follow me,' the angel said. Peter followed the angel past the first guard and the second and then the locked gates of the prison swung open in front of them. When Peter was safely out in the street and away from the prison, the angel left him.

357
A knocking at the door
Acts 12:12–17

'Bang! Bang! Bang!' Rhoda went to answer the door of the house where Peter's friends were gathered. When she recognised Peter's voice, she was so excited that she ran to tell the others he was there without opening the door. 'Don't be silly,' they told her. 'It can't be Peter.' But the knocking went on until they opened the door and Peter came in! Peter explained what had happened. God had answered their prayers with a miracle.

358
A new disciple
Acts 16:9–15

Saul by this time was a changed man. Once he had met Jesus on the road to Damascus, everything was different. He had regained his sight and become one of the Christians he had once hated. People now called him Paul. And he was so happy to know Jesus that he told everyone he knew about him, travelling from place to place. A businesswoman named Lydia heard Paul preaching in a place called Philippi and asked to be baptised. She was one of many!

359
Paul in trouble!
Acts 16:16–25

In Macedonia, a slave girl made her masters rich by telling fortunes. Paul was travelling with Silas when he met her and set her free of the evil spirit inside her—but then she could no longer see the future. Her masters were so angry that Paul and Silas were beaten and thrown into prison. Paul was not stopped so easily. He praised God and sang hymns there just as he did when he was not in prison.

360
A miracle in the prison cell
Acts 16:26–40

Suddenly there was an earthquake and the chains fell off Paul's hands, just as they had fallen from Peter's. The prison guard was so sure Paul and Silas would escape in the darkness, he drew his sword to kill himself. 'Stop!' Paul shouted. 'We are all here!' 'But how can I be saved?' said the guard. 'Trust Jesus and be baptised!' Paul answered. So the guard and all his family became Christians. They bathed Paul and Silas' wounds and took care of them.

361
Paul's journeys
Acts 16—20

Paul and Silas were released from prison and went to stay with Lydia for a while. But Paul could not stay still for long. He spent many years travelling, teaching people wherever he went. He told people that God loved them so much that he had sent Jesus to die on a cross for them. He encouraged them to come and ask Jesus for the free gift of life that God gave to all who knew they needed his help. Everywhere Paul went, people believed his message and wanted to be baptised. New Christian churches were started in many different countries. The message Jesus had given to his disciples was spreading everywhere.

362
Paul's sufferings
Acts 21:15—26:32

Paul had no real home. Sometimes people threw stones at him and left him battered and bruised. Once he was left so hurt that his friends thought he was dead. In some places he was welcomed but often people drove him away. He suffered many bad things as he travelled from country to country. But nothing would stop Paul from taking the message of Jesus to people. When he went home to Jerusalem, he was arrested and imprisoned for years. Eventually, as he was a Roman citizen, Paul asked to see the emperor in Rome.

363
The violent storm
Acts 27:1—20

Luke, the doctor, travelled with Paul on the ship that took him to Rome. They left at a bad time of year and Paul tried to warn them to wait until the weather was better. No one listened. At first the sea was calm but soon a violent wind tossed the ship around. Waves lashed at the deck and no sun, moon or stars could be seen. The sailors were terrified. They threw the cargo overboard and anything else they did not need, but still they were tossed about in the storm. They had gone days without food. 'Don't give up,' Paul told them. 'God will not let us die.'

364
Shipwrecked!
Acts 27:21—28:1

Eventually they saw land and a sandy bay. But the ship got stuck on a sand bank and part of it broke up. They reached the shore by swimming or clinging to parts of the broken ship and drifting in on the tide. They had reached the island of Malta. All 276 people on the boat finally made it to the shore, where they were looked after by the people of Malta. While they were there, waiting for better weather and another ship, Paul prayed for people and healed them of their diseases. During the three months that they were there, many more people learned about Jesus.

365
Paul writes from Rome

Acts 28:11–31

When they finally reached Rome, Paul was allowed to stay in a house with a soldier to guard him. Many people there would come to him to ask about the Christian faith and together they discussed what the scriptures said about Jesus. Some people were convinced and became Christians; others did not. Paul spent two years there in this way and wrote letters to Christians in all the countries he had visited, helping them with the questions they had about their faith and encouraging them to follow Jesus.